Thus Spoke The Plant

A Remarkable Journey Of Groundbreaking Scientific Discoveries And Personal Encounters With Plants

Monica Gagliano, PhD

EasyRead Large

Read How You Want

LARGE PRINT BOOKS, BRAILLE & DAISY

Copyright Page from the Original Book

Published by
North Atlantic Books
Berkeley, California

Cover photo © HNK/Shutterstock.com
Cover design by Jasmine Hromjak
Book design by Happenstance Type-O-Rama

Printed in the United States of America

Thus Spoke the Plant: A Remarkable Journey of Groundbreaking Scientific Discoveries and Personal Encounters with Plants is sponsored and published by the Society for the Study of Native Arts and Sciences (dba North Atlantic Books), an educational nonprofit based in Berkeley, California, that collaborates with partners to develop cross-cultural perspectives, nurture holistic views of art, science, the humanities, and healing, and seed personal and global transformation by publishing work on the relationship of body, spirit, and nature.

North Atlantic Books' publications are available through most bookstores. For further information, visit our website at www.northatlanticbooks.com or call 800-733-3000.

Library of Congress Cataloging-in-Publication Data

Names: Gagliano, Monica, 1976- author.
Title: Thus spoke the plant : a remarkable journey of groundbreaking scientific discoveries and personal encounters with plants / Monica Gagliano.
Description: Berkeley, California : North Atlantic Books, [2018] | Includes index.
Identifiers: LCCN 2018024075 (print) | LCCN 2018026039 (ebook)

Subjects: LCSH: Human-plant relationships—Anecdotes. | Plants—Anecdotes.
Classification: LCC QK46.5.H85 (ebook) | LCC QK46.5.H85 G34 2018 (print) | DDC 581—dc23
LC record available at https://lccn.loc.gov/2018024075

1 2 3 4 5 6 7 8 9 KPC 22 21 20 19 18

Printed on recycled paper

North Atlantic Books is committed to the protection of our environment.
We partner with FSC-certified printers using soy-based inks
and print on recycled paper whenever possible.

TABLE OF CONTENTS

To Humanity

The Void sings everything into Being.
You are the Singing Void.
Then Sing!

FOREWORD

Walk in nature—anywhere in the world—and open your senses. Not just one or two of the five, but *all* of them. The sounds of the lofty tree crowns swaying in the breeze, the sight of deep green that soothes your soul, the smell of soil and bark and the breath of oxygen that rushes into your lungs, the feel of soft leaves as they brush your hands, the taste of sweet fruit on your lips. Monica Gagliano, in *Thus Spoke the Plant,* asks you to open up to the possibility that plants have some of the same senses—the ability to hear, see, smell, feel, and taste—along with distinct modalities, new dimensions, to make sense of their world, such as detecting electromagnetic fields, sounds, and low-voltage vibrations. Then check in with your own circle of awareness—your mind, heart, soul, and body. Not just your five senses, but also your spirit. You have multiple modalities, too, like the plants. And, chances are, they are more aligned than before you stepped outside. Your mind calms, your heart fills, your soul is soothed, and your body feels vibrantly *alive.* You feel whole, more connected inside, and more attuned to the world. You feel the power to act in your own life and to help craft a more evolved society, one that is connected and attuned to itself and to nature.

Most of us recognize the essential role of plants in our well-being, in the very breath we take. Plants helped create an oxygenated atmosphere, enabling the eventual evolution of humans. The evolution of plants has been so successful that today they account for over 99 percent of the living biomass on Earth. The presence of humans and other animals is dwarfed in comparison. Still, we humans walk through nature not seeing plants as highly evolved creatures, but rather as inanimate, passive, and inferior species. We have constructed a simple vision of plants as lacking in intelligence, agency, or sentience. We have relegated them to the lowest rung of a hierarchy that is headed by humans.

This human construct ignores evolutionary history and has shaped our scientific questions and limited us to finding only certain answers about the meaning of our lives. And from this superiority complex, we have justified the global abuse of plants. And not just of plants, but of any creature we consider inferior to humans—which means all species. Of course, not all cultures have this anthropocentric superiority complex, but the most dominant and powerful one on Earth today does, and this has created multiple crises on a global scale. Averting socio-ecological disaster now will take a scientific revolution. It will take a deconstruction of our reductionist and parochial approach to understanding life and the invention of whole new ways of understanding the world.

In *Thus Spoke the Plant,* Monica Gagliano will provide you with a completely different way of understanding and knowing the world. Not just the plant world, but your whole world view. She asks that you tear off your lifetime of cultural blinders and open all of your senses to let in the world of plants. To help you do this, she takes you on her personal journey of confronting her own biases, which started with her changing careers, listening to her dreams, and then acting on her intuition to speak with the plant people that visit her with the guidance of indigenous seers. The plant people call on her to be their voice and guide her to understand their cognitive powers. This personal and professional journey leads her to ask brilliant questions and design simple, elegant experiments that uncover new modalities in plant intelligence. We learn that plants can communicate, are capable of learning, have memory, make decisions, and are cognizant of a greater purpose, in addition to their own Darwinian success, to the communities in which they live.

In Monica Gagliano, plants have chosen the most open, inquisitive, brilliant mind as their spokesperson. With her feet firmly planted in both the scientific method and the wisdom of plants, Monica has tapped into the multidimensionality of nature that will break down forever our suffocating parochialism about our environment. In the face of repeated rejection of her papers by the scientific establishment, she has persisted and published her experiments in the top plant ecology journals. We owe her a debt of gratitude for swimming against the tide and opening up our awareness, even as the rip currents tried to pull her under.

I first met Monica Gagliano in 2016 at a think tank on plant communication hosted by the Bill and Melinda Gates Foundation in Seattle. About thirty leading scientists in the field of plant communication had gathered together to discuss how their discoveries could inform sustainable agricultural around the world. Monica's youth, in particular, masked a wisdom and body of work that most scientists never attain. I had just shown my work on mycorrhizal fungal networks that link mother trees with the myriad other trees and plants in the forest and how the Aboriginal people of North America have long known of their importance to forest health. Many brilliant presentations followed, but what I remember most was Monica standing up for proper attribution of companion-plant communities to the first peoples of the Americas, rather than to new industrial scientific patents. Monica, having journeyed deeply with them, was standing up for the native plants and the people.

In asking us to open all of our senses and to embrace new ones we haven't even explored before, Monica, through her personal stories and scientific discoveries, has opened a path through the woods for us to follow. *Thus Spoke the Plant* is more than about scientific discovery—it is about a revolution that will compel us to see the world through a completely new lens and will motivate us to change our attitudes, behaviors, and actions so that we can alter the course of the socio-environmental crises we have created. So open your mind, set aside your biases, and be prepared to change your view of the world and your place in it—forever.

DR. SUZANNE SIMARD
Professor of Forest Ecology
The University of British Columbia
June 25, 2018

PRELUDE

Keep looking for Truth in the wrong places, and you will never find it.
Stop looking there, out there. Find Truth here, where Truth resides.

I have always loved stories, but then who doesn't? Infinite in numbers, stories continually grow within and all around us, which may be why they seem to be with us wherever we go. Some capture us with their lies, others shock us with their truths, and still others inspire us immensely with their courage. No matter the myriad nuanced colors, all stories are luminous threads that weave us into the tapestry of life, vibrant filaments that bring our world into being and then undo it. The stories you will encounter in this book unspool a thread that invites you to reclaim a far more profound level of perceiving the world than the one you may have so long been accustomed to. Perhaps they will open a window onto the greener vista you had forgotten was there.

But let's be clear—this is no flight of fancy. While I admit that some of the adventures and occurrences described in the following pages will, at least to some, appear weird, out of the ordinary, or totally unbelievable, this is not a work of fiction or a handed-down imaginary tale I am asking you to believe in. This is a real and sober firsthand account of my scientific research probing into the vegetal kingdom over the last decade. By taking you behind the scenes of academic science and describing the inner workings of a research journey that reveals the dynamic role plants played in instigating a new formulation of contemporary science, this is a powerful story about the unexpected and yet remarkable encounter between scientific insight and plant wisdom. Such an encounter takes place at the frontier, where the physical world as (we think) we know it and alternate domains of reality (weirder than we can conceive of) meet. Here the ordinary and the peculiar go hand in hand and, at times, bump into each other to set a whole world alight with new, even paradoxical, possibilities.

I arrived in this new world amid the daunting dread of what I might lose and the irrepressible curiosity of what I might find, both professionally and personally. Nobody told me that I would have to do a complete summersault flip, leaving my ideas of the "normal" behind and leaping into the unknown, or that I would land on solid ground, with one foot in each world and yet together. At first, this was a traumatic experience and a dangerous state of affairs—it is terrifying to lose your footing as you walk on a thin slippery line that meanders its way in and out of different perceptual landscapes where chances must be taken, and must be taken with no handrails to hold on to! Though what seemed an impossible feat—the marriage between the objectivity of the scientific method and knowledge and the subjectivity of transcendental experiences and intuition—not only proved to be absolutely possible but a most incredibly profound and exciting coup.

This book endeavors to take *you* to that world. Oh, don't be afraid. You are not asked to subscribe to a particular doctrine or to agree with quixotic beliefs. Quite the opposite—put all beliefs, cultural assumptions, judgments, and prejudices aside, and just listen. And if you need to, you can call me crazy, but do yourself a favor, and resist the temptation to dismiss this story as impossible before you take a leap outside the box of your "normal" and allow for the magical absurdity of your subjective experience to walk alongside the objective rationality of your logical mind. This book is about how I learned to trust them both and where that led me.

When the End Is the Beginning

This book is about plants, but its story began not with them, but with an animal. It was a small tropical fish living in the colorful waters of the Great Barrier Reef, where circumstances that were normal one moment turned inexplicably strange the next. At that critical juncture, everything changed for me, and the world ceased to be what I had been taught it was. Here is what happened.

Much of my earlier professional life could be described as "water in water"—the waters of the human body immersed in the big waters of the earth's body. Given my research training in marine animal ecology, I spent years breathing under the surface in the waters of the Great Barrier Reef, the largest coral reef in the world and the only natural phenomenon visible from space, to study the private life of a little damselfish species, commonly known as the Ambon damselfish but formally named *Pomacentrus amboinensis.* During the hot Australian summer months, I spent countless research hours observing the Ambon females laying eggs in perfect little nooks within the complexity of the reef structure and the males aggressively protecting these benthic nests from egg predators and other intruders. The eggs remain under watchful paternal eyes for only a few days before hatching. Then, under the bright light of a full moon and equipped with one big nutritious yolk sac Mum had packed for them, the tiny larvae wriggle their way out of the nest and away, immediately embarking in a courageous journey far from the reef and out in the open ocean. And only a handful will survive to swim all the way back home to the reef. Here, as time progresses, the transparent baby fish will turn into confident bright yellow youngsters who will audaciously venture farther and farther out from the safety of their hidey-hole to catch some plankton in the water or compete over new prime spots in the coralline estate. And before you know it, bright yellow bodies of different hues, sizes, and ages are flickering in the water column like wild confetti! Their presence feels like a true miracle, a celebration of life.

Today, this pondering fills me with a great sense of awe. At the time, however, when this species was the main object of my scientific research, their commitment to life didn't stop me from fulfilling the murderous necessity of science. It was so until the fish ceased to be an anonymous data point on a spreadsheet, just another "fish" in the agreed sense of the word—the human-centered categorical boundaries asserted through to the Linnaean classification system, a fiction brought into being by a particular worldview. Once it was no longer an elusive entity void of individuality, the *object* of my research became a *subject* for my learning. And everything changed.

I remember that morning vividly. I had been in the water every day for months, monitoring the reproductive output of wild *P. amboinensis* pairs. Every day, we encountered each other at the edge, where the safety of the reef ended and my hand stretched out, opened. A week into the study, these wild animals snuggled inside that hand as my fingers gently curled around their scaly bodies and then opened again. They knew me, personally. I knew them, one by one. On the last day of the study, I went in the water with the intention of saying goodbye before returning in the afternoon to capture and, as per protocol, kill them all. I remember that morning. No one was in sight; no one was approaching me, let alone my open hand. A chilling sensation filled me. In that moment, I knew they knew. I felt the blood of all the past killings I had done in the name of my science, and a dreadful feeling of guilt flooded my heart. Frozen and not knowing what to do, I did what I knew. That afternoon, I went back in the water with nets and catch bags and killed them all. I understand now that theirs was an incredible sacrifice that delivered the one gift that would change everything. Because through the intimacy of our encounter, the time spent being together and being with each other had broken down the taxonomic boundary. In this permeability, a true nakedness had emerged, the kind of vulnerability necessary to establish openness. They taught me empathy. They taught me kinship and communion. And I never killed again.[1]

This all happened in 2008, a year that kick-started a great professional (and personal) watershed. I was a postdoctoral research fellow in climate change ecology at James Cook University back then. Because of this experience I had on the reef, I had developed a profound internal conflict sparked by the realization that, for me, there was no scientific question significant or exceptional enough that could justify the killing of another living being. This was immediately followed by the horrifying problem of how to continue doing my scientific research without the slaughter. I tried to, and it was not good enough—in the temple of modern science, a blood sacrifice to the old gods of the Enlightenment is still, for the most part, the required ceremonial procedure. So without realizing that *I* was to be the sacrificial offering this time around, I fumbled in futile attempts to desperately hold together what had already come undone, what had simply run its course. At the time, I was still unaware of the fact that my research career as an animal scientist had just ended and a new one as the plant scientist was about to start. I was also unaware of the fact that an invitation from the vegetal world had already been extended. And, certainly, I was yet to realize that the plants would not only come to rescue my career but also radically transmute it by re-enchanting both the rationally empowered mind of scientist and the awe-inspired heart of the human that dwelled within me. Indeed, my professional and personal life were about to take an incredible and wild turn as I staggered along an unfamiliar territory and, like Alice, found myself tumbling down a rather strange rabbit hole.

This book is about what I found down that rabbit hole. It is about the up-close-and-personal encounters with the plants themselves—as well as with plant shamans, indigenous elders, and mystics from around the world—and about how these experiences were integrated with an incredible research journey and the groundbreaking scientific discoveries that emerged from it, so as to relate this new advanced knowledge to modern culture. This book offers you a fresh, imaginative space for reconceiving the connections between plants and humanity and contemplating improved human-to-nonhuman habits of living on this planet as part of a whole. It is time.

Attunement to Green Symphonies

This book is *about* plants and *by* plants. It is a phytobiography—a collection of stories, each written together with and on behalf of a plant person. These stories are told through the narrative voice of both the human and the plant person, through the language *of* plants and my language *for* them. But let me be clear on this most delicate subject. There is no attempt at, or need for, ventriloquizing by assigning a voice to plants or speaking for them to render these stories intelligible to our human mind. Here, the human is not an interpreter who translates a mental representation in her head as if it were plant-speak and then puts it into words we can comprehend or scribbles it on a page we know how to read. Rather, the human is a listener who filters out personal noise to hear plants speak, who engages in active dialog with these nonhuman intelligences, which are far more real than our current scientific constructs allow us to contend with. Here, the human acts as a coauthor who physically delivers those conversations to the page. As such, these stories emerge out of a human-plant collaborative endeavor and a mixed writing style, which I think we can fittingly call *plant-writing.*

Through plant-writing, this book transcends the view of plants as the objects of scientific materialism and empowers a new and yet timeless vision of the world, one in which we encounter plants as the persons and companions they are and in which we bring kind-heartedness to each encounter. By weaving these plant-human stories together into a magical journey of discovery and interconnectedness, this book reaffirms the precious gift our partnership with plants has been throughout the evolutionary history of our species and our search for understanding who we are and what are we here for. On this regard, I suspect that anyone who dares embarking on such a search will eventually find these answers. The stories of how each one of us may find the answers will differ widely, each story being marvelously tailor-made to suit our individual taste. However, the actual answers probably won't. So while these are my stories tracking what happened to me in my life as a professional scientist in search of my answers on what is the essence of our human experience, this book is about anyone else as much as it is about me, and these stories belong to all of us as much as they do to me. These are our stories of what it takes to stay aligned with a greater vision and go though the process of bringing it to life in the world. These stories belong to the heart of our humanity, encoded with the memories of our species and all the life forms we descended from. Like in a magnificent orchestral symphony, each story is notated separately for individual plants, and still, all stories are sounding together to remind us of our deep history of connection to and interdependence with all others (humans and nonhumans) and to reconnect our magnificent minds with our precious hearts so we dare to dream a truly inspiring future for the whole.

Chapter O

Listen, then you may hear something being spoken.

~ Oryngham ~

Oryngham means thank you for listening in the language of the plants. It is not a word, as we humans understand it, because its meaning cannot be spoken—nor can it be heard. However, we can experience it by feeling with our bodies and listening to what our ears cannot hear. When we learn to listen to plants without the need to hear them speak, a language that we have forgotten emerges; it is a language beyond words, one that does not wander or pretend or mislead. It is a language that conveys its rich and meaningful expression by bypassing the household of our mind and directly connecting one spirit to another. This language belongs to plants, and so do these stories.

This story starts from the middle. The middle is a swinging hammock hanging barely above the wooden floor of a small stilt hut. With its typical thatched hipped roof, walls of a pastel blue color, decorated with the intricate geometric patterns distinctive of the Shipibo people of the Amazon lowlands of Peru, this is the hut of my dreams. I had dreamt of this exact place a few months earlier, back home in Australia. On the first night, I had dreamt of standing by the outside of a small hut, noticing the black labyrinthine patterns painted on its walls. The little door was wide open and the entrance pitch-black. Climbing up three little wooden steps was all that was required to enter, a truly simple task unless one came face-to-face with a gatekeeper. As the yellow-green eyes of a black jaguar emerged shimmering out of the darkness of the doorway and pierced deeply into mine, I woke up. The same scene materialized on the following night, but with no feline warden in sight. I peered inside the hut and was surprised to see a fire burning in the middle of the room and a young man tending it. The fire keeper gestured me to sit by the fire to face him, and so I did. As the orange and yellow flames danced in the space between us, the man instructed me to sing. Despite my most sincere efforts, no sound ever came out of me, and I woke up. The following night, I sat at the fire with a much older man in Shipibo dress. He was grinning at me with a flicker of satisfaction in his dark, narrow eyes as I sang a bizarre tune made of sounds I could not hear and meanings I could not speak. I woke up that morning knowing that somewhere that hut, that man, and those strange songs were waiting for me. This is how Socoba, a tropical tree also known as Bellaco-caspi *(Himatanthus sucuuba),* quite literally, called me to the outskirts of Pucallpa. So a few months later I set off for Peru.

Almost thirty-five feet tall, Socoba stands tall and proud with a crown of perfumed white flowers adorning her head of brilliant green foliage. She breathes up high in the sky, while her feet are firmly held in a moist, at times flooded, ground, just like the humans she dwells with. Here, the Earth secures the roots of both Socoba and the Shipibo people, and the Cosmos, unconcerned by the specific nature of their complexion, inscribes itself onto their skin.[1] The Shipibo wear the cosmic patterns of meandering lines and hidden luminous harmonies on their painted faces and bodies. Likewise, Socoba wears them as a ceremonial dress of rough, mottled bark. As these cosmic inscriptions pierce through the very skin tasked with keeping the outside world out and all of the insides in, the worlds beyond this world emerge, percolating in to be carefully mapped out. It is at the skin that the tree and the shaman meet, a crossroad of sacred offerings where a wound is etched in the body of one to heal that of the other.[2]

The Socoba tree stretches her arboreal arms to the sky and over the *maloka* (ceremonial hut), the beautifully painted temple space where Don M—the Shipibo man I had seen in my dream—conducts his healing ceremonies and curative rituals as the *maestro vegetalista* (plant shaman) for the local community. Don M had told me that Socoba called him that morning, soon after my arrival at his home. He had heeded her call and met her whistling one of those strange tunes while swirling in the air around her torso white puffs of sacred jungle tobacco, or *mapacho,* as Amazonian shamans call *Nicotiana rustica.*[3] Socoba had informed him of how she had come to my dreams to call me to this place to work with her. Then she proceeded to gift him some of her bark so he could prepare a concoction for me. As the highly respected *planta maestra* that she is, Socoba was committed to teach me about herself as a nifty healer of the physical as well as emotional and spiritual body. To open this plant teacher–human student dialogue, all I needed to do was to follow the *dieta,*[4] a time during which I was to ingest the plant regularly while in isolation, observing total sexual abstinence and an uninspiring diet of unseasoned vegetables and rice. So I drank the concoction made from her bark that night—and the following night too—as Socoba swiftly aligned with my present and quietly befriended my past. And I drank her again and again for the following weeks of my apprenticeship, while in a hammock that swung barely off the wooden floor of the little hut I had dreamt of months before, lying in my own bed half a world away.

The first time Socoba showed herself to me, I completely failed to recognize her. The night I started dieting with her, Don M recommended paying attention to my dreams, where she was most likely to first reveal her presence. I certainly had a good sleep that first night she came to visit, but I noticed nothing in particular that I would have associated to her, well, except for one image. It consisted of a dark blood-red background with thick black lines, a simple image that had kept popping up throughout the night. Like the intermission of bygone films was needed to facilitate the changing of reels, this image appeared like a wide screen, creating a momentary pause between one dream and the next. The following afternoon, the same image materialized on the white paper of my drawing pad with a clear message—*todas las cosas estan juntas* (all things are connected). I suddenly understood what Socoba was saying—"it is through blood that everything is connected."

In that moment, I knew without knowing that Socoba was a blood cleanser, the healer of conditions that affected the blood and the network of vessels that assure the smooth flowing of blood inside the human body. This is how Socoba articulated her initial insights and instructed me on what I would later read in the scientific literature. In fact, decades of pharmacological research have confirmed her positive effects on the vascular system. She regulates the numbers of red blood cells and oxygen-carrying hemoglobins—deficiencies of which lead to anemia—and maintains healthy blood pressure and the permeability of blood vessels, which makes her a potent healer of several inflammation-related diseases ranging from simple hay fever to life-threatening sepsis, atherosclerosis, and cancer.[5]

At once, the whole situation had become absurd, hysterical, and liberating. Why invest millennia in a blind and, quite frankly, dangerous trail-and-error process (as suggested by most scholars) when, in just a few weeks or months, one can learn about the therapeutic properties of plants straight from the (vegetal!) horse's mouth? Why insist on denying the ability of plants to *speak* to us and even teach us when that is what they have done for, well, millennia?[6] The claim that plants (and nature in general) have no voice and no teaching for us is rooted in ancient history, dating back to Socrates, who declared that trees could teach him nothing but then, ironically, reminded us of prophecies uttered by old oak trees (all the while, resting comfortably on a soft patch of grass under the shade of a majestic plane tree on a sizzling summer's day).[7] This schizophrenic discrepancy has haunted Western thinking throughout its history—accrediting a voice to plants and even acknowledging them as wise oracles and teachers, only to take it all away in the next breath. Despite the numerous attempts to repudiate or, worst, denigrate that which sophisticated Western thinking has defined as ignorant and superstitious, a simple fact remains—the vegetal world never stopped teaching humans, reaching to us through our dreams and visions, and we never stopped learning by listening to it.

In the light of evolution, learning by listening to plants must have served us well and afforded us major selective benefits. Those who cared to listen would have been less likely to make dreadful mistakes while distinguishing which plants were edible and beneficial. Because their approach was far from ignorant—being well informed by the plants themselves—those who listened would have been able to test and apply their newly acquired knowledge straightaway. (Just think about it, a random trial-and-error approach would have taken a long time and cost lots of lives before any useful and practical information could be revealed to us!) Of course, learning by listening did not eliminate the fact that the process of discovering, remembering, and sharing a vast amount of information about medicinal plants still would have been accompanied by a huge cognitive inventory of their therapeutic properties. Our mind would have had to managed this complexity, perhaps by dividing up the information into smaller morsels, sets of distinguishable qualities that best represented a therapeutic property. These classifications would have served us as powerful mnemonic devices to prop up the finite capacity of our memory. But what a relief to know that none of it could ever be forgotten! What a relief to know that these enormous vegetal archives would always be open for consultation. Plant knowledge is *in* and *with* the plants themselves, never lost, always available to those who listen.

Indeed, plants seem to know us well and what we need. In some herbalistic circles, it is said that plants are willing to help us and are keen to share their knowledge with us.[8] As plants continue to coevolve with humans (and other animal species), it is also suggested that new properties and functions for plants will emerge as new needs develop.[9] The obvious question, then, is not so much about whether or even what they know, but *how* and *why* they do. From a utilitarian perspective, it is, of course, valuable to know that a plant like Socoba can be used to treat conditions that affect the circulatory system. But how does an Amazonian tree like Socoba know about the functioning of the human body and the healing of its dysfunctions? And why would she hold such an understanding? Answers cannot be given to questions that we are not ready to ask, and at the time, these questions never even occurred to me. They materialized only when I began writing this phytobiographical account of Socoba six years later. Then, like a dog with a bone, my unrelenting mind was hungry for the impossible answers to these bizarre, even unbearable questions. I simply had no idea, but to think that the riddle could be solved by virtue of a merely mental workout was the real fallacy. Instead, it all happened effortlessly. As the questions emerged, the answers did too. This is when Socoba woke me up in the early hours of the day to elucidate them. And her answer was as natural and light as oxygen.

During my *dieta* with her, Socoba had spoken clearly about everything being connected through blood. Now, so many years later, she was unwrapping this earlier insight like a sweet candy to convey the teaching that, in actuality, mattered the most. Don M had told me that once dieted, a plant is a teacher that will stay with you forever and keep teaching you in her own plant time; because of that, there is no need to diet the same plant twice. And indeed, Socoba was vibrating inside my body, moving ever so lightly to remind me of her indisputable presence. And like that first night of my *dieta* back in Peru, she displayed her mastery as a teacher by revealing that "the wisdom is in the oxygen, and the blood is the great connector." Speaking without words, she went on showing me how—this way and that through the vascular system—blood carries oxygen to the main hectic hubs of the body, as well as to its more secluded and quieter locations. This is possible because red blood cells are packed with hemoglobin, whose job is to trap the oxygen available in the lungs and transport the precious atoms into the tissues of the body[10] and, from there, to freight carbon dioxide molecules back to the lungs, where they can be released. At each inhalation, free oxygen breathed out by plants enters us in all its levity and allows us to convert what we eat into energy. At each exhalation, we let go of carbon dioxide and water, which plants ingeniously combine with a touch of sunlight to make their own food and, once again, more oxygen. Excitedly, she continued by pointing out how we breathe each other in and out of existence, one made by the exhalation of the other.

Arising from perfect stillness, this deep breath of fresh air is the necessary movement that brings innovation and the expression of individuality, where the unique and the separate as the plant and the human are made temporarily possible. And this same inspired movement that generated them also unbinds them, incessantly releasing both the plant and the human into a space where the separate parts are dissolved. With every breath, then, the plant knows the human as herself. At every breath, the human becomes more plant-like than he realizes, and given the right circumstances, he recognizes how he too *knows* the plant as himself. Here Socoba vanished, leaving me in my bed to fall asleep again.

How can a plant readily know us when we are hardly aware of the plantness within ourselves? The theoretical notion of a plantness reverberating within the human body has been contemplated since ancient times.[11] Perceived through the veil of motionlessness even by our most brilliant minds, this plantness has seemed inaccessible and even deliberately hidden from us.[12] Well, that is true when we try to *think* of it. It is because of its *unthinkability*—in the sense that it cannot be comprehended in a conceptual way—that only the experience of *feeling* it (by virtue of the patterns of information that it delivers) makes it real. When we feel it, this plantness is allowed to emanate unconcealed within us at all times. What appeared to be intangible—an obscure otherness—is unveiled as the intimate familiarity of an obvious and luminous likeness. And far from being impenetrable and distant, the plant is revealed as unquestionably open. Literally. As philosopher Michael Marder puts it, "the plant, of course, does not ask what water is, and it has no 'idea' of water as a distinct object."[13] Because, in her vegetal openness, the plant is not separate from the exteriority of her milieu. And as elaborated directly by Socoba, the plant exists in a state of open communion in which the fiction of personalized boundaries collapses.

In her grounded experience of life, she needs neither questions nor concepts of water to know water. In fact, she does not need to ask anything at all to know. This is how the plant knows the other; this is how she knows the human as herself. This knowing comes from being empty, but emptiness does not reduce the plant to a passive, spirit-less, and objectified materiality (and we will consider the implications of this later) but rather liberates her vitality from the pursuit of fulfillment. Already fulfilled in every moment, always realized in her full potential, the plant is completely available to know her circumstances by listening deeply. For a human being to know this way is to be (at least momentarily) free from internal inconsistencies between attitudes and actions. It means to be empty of the socially indoctrinated belief system that prescribes the boundaries of how we are expected to perceive and behave in a given situation and that justifies our actions even when they are unwise and out of sorts with our internal emotional and moral intelligence.

As the preconceived ideas and judgments we make about the other are abandoned, we are finally available to listen to our circumstances as they present themselves in each moment. Then, as Socoba pointed out, we are open to know the other as ourselves. This way of knowing is not ephemeral, but earthly and concrete. This availability to truly listen by feeling the other as we meet is not empathy, which bears upon the empathizer projecting and depositing himself into the other in order to rediscover himself—a form of narcissism that makes the other a sort of imaginative variation of the empathizer.[14] Instead, knowing by deep listening has the quality of a perfect surprise, pertinent to the moment of the encounter, not conditioned by anything inside one or the other and, thus, not intentionally predetermined.[15]

The openness to this deep listening is oxygenated in the natural body made of blood and bones (or sap and fibers), where skins and barks are no longer perceived as functional boundaries that separate the inner and outer, containing us. As it emerges from and merges into the space where one encounters the other, this openness reveals our participation in the communion with each other. Because the openness of plant being constantly invites our openness to being humans, our encounter with plants confronts us with the limits of our capacity for such embodied listening and active participation. Thus, plants come to represent the marker points of our resistance to transcend our narcissistic and anthropocentric propensities toward exceptionalism, a necessary requirement for entering such space. This was the teaching that Socoba, the plant, had come to share with me, the human. But that was not all. So let's retrace our steps back to Socoba and her arboreal arms stretched out and over the *maloka* with the beautiful Shipibo designs snaking across its walls, somewhere outside Pucallpa.

The tapping noise of a happy beak came from the door of my hut. I opened it, looked out, and then down. And there was my feathered visitor, chest puffed up with attitude in his shimmering green tuxedo, waiting. Pedrito, a bright green little parrot, had knocked at my door and come visiting almost every day since I had started my *dieta* with Socoba. As I opened the door, he tilted his head to one side, looking up at me with deceitful timidness. He was waiting to be welcomed in. What a funny sight—leaning his body forward, with his feathery arms folded behind his back like an old Zen master immersed in the deep contemplation of life, Pedrito would waste no time trotting inside to make himself at home. After a brief inspection of the colorful pencils left unorganized on top of my drawing pad and what little else was lying around on the wooden floor of the hut, he would flutter up to sit on the rope holding one side of my hammock and wait for me to get comfortable in it. Cocooned in a reality suspended off the floor of this world but still connected to it by a few ropes, Pedrito and I would swing together across the universe of our minds.

That day, we were lulled back and forth by the calming sound of his beak clicking and grinding as he fell asleep in the fold of my arm. I stared outside through the open door of my hut and across the naked space between huts, where I could see the exposed "shower"—a solitary rusty pipe spouting water out of the ground, nonstop—which I made use of, albeit reluctantly and only out of sheer necessity. While swinging to the calming sound of Pedrito in the shelter of my hammock, I stared outside past the open shower and over the loud music and the racket of human life engrossed with itself. And further, my gaze traveled across the hushed movement of an other-than-human world connecting me to Socoba. From my vantage point, I could see Socoba peacefully shining in the sun as she stretched up and over the *maloka* where we were to meet in ceremony after nightfall. But Socoba's silent and motionless appearance was deceptive. She had no intention of waiting till nightfall before bearing her next teaching session on the perception of reality.

While in plain sight, everything disappeared for a while for me that afternoon. The noise from outside evaporated. The hut and the hammock I was swinging in dissolved, although I was still there. Pedrito also vanished, though he was still asleep in my arms. I had not moved, and my eyes were wide open, but what I was seeing was somewhere not there. Socoba was there.

"Ah, you got it!" she said without words. Without words, I asked, "I got it—what?" and then I saw the answer: a bright, shiny road. At the verge of this luminous road, I saw all of the people I have ever stumbled upon. Every single one of them was there—the woman at the deli shop where I used to buy sweets (and, at times, shoplift chocolate bars) after school; a ticket inspector on a morning train that was traveling to my hometown; a neighbor whom I have only ever nodded and smiled at as I walked past with my dog—all of the people who mattered to me, as well as those I never thought of consequence to my life, all of the people who ever loved me, as well as those who never seemed to. Applauding and cheering loudly "you got it!"—so thrilled, so pleased—they had all converged from divergent timelines and eclectic spaces into that moment, out of sequence with time and space. I was staggered.

Even now, as I recall the event, I can still feel the confusion I felt then and, at once, the sensation of something miraculous happening in the underbelly of a reality we mostly agree to deny, but which I was peering into. As I recall the event, I am also aware that my words appear to carry the hallmarks of egomania, or at least a good dose of delusional grandeur. And rest assured that I did doubt my own sanity many times, especially when all of these odd occurrences started—and yet I know I do not suffer from psychoses, and certainly not from a messianic complex. This is simply the event as I remember it, knowing that even my current recalling and understanding of it is likely incomplete.

As I walked toward a bright light ahead, passing the crowd like an Oscars celebrity on the red carpet, Socoba explained how each one of them played the role I had scripted for them as part of the "story of me" that I directed. "Look at those who put their hands up to play a challenging character, knowing that you would loathe it, judging it bitterly and unforgivingly." She pressed on, "See those you thought were out to hurt you? They played their assigned roles with great perfection and infinite patience, for your benefit alone. Their choice was made out of love alone. And out of this love, all agreed to be part of your play, so you could walk to this point and remember the radiance of the light that is *you.*"

Overwhelmed by a profound sense of gratitude I had not known before and an intense love radiating from everyone around me, I was now sobbing, uncontrollably, like a small child. Every person had brought a unique aspect to my story that would allow me to express a distinctive facet of myself. Could I possibly be the only character in my life who was unaware that this was just a wonderful performance? Was I the *un*knowing star of my own spellbinding play? "You see, child, you got it!" Socoba reassured me, while I raised my left hand up—it was not my own adult hand, but that of a child. The road of light was leading forward to the beginning, a point of origin where all timelines and dreamscapes joined. Here, each individual character merged and disappeared into the light with me—spontaneously, effortlessly. This was the space where, as Socoba had already revealed in an earlier teaching, the separate parts, now liberated, dissolved and unified.

It was nightfall by the time Don M came to fetch me for the ceremony. Stunned by the bewildering events of that afternoon, my walk over to the *maloka* was, without a doubt, a clumsy one. Before entering the ceremonial hut, I looked up at the Socoba tree peacefully shining in the moonlight just as much as she had done earlier in the sunlight. I entered the *maloka,* sat down on the mattress placed on the floor for me, and cringed at the off-putting fizz of fermentation exhaled by a small plastic bottle Don M had just opened. Homemade and organic, the content was no lemonade soda, but the powerful psychedelic Ayahuasca *medicina,*[16] the acrid brew he had prepared a few weeks ago, just before my arrival. *Mapacho* already hanging off his lip, Don M looked up at me with the exact same grin I had seen on his face when I first saw him, so many months before, in the dream that had brought me here. Before I could plead to Socoba and the plant spirits for a gentle ride, Don M had handed me a double dose of the *medicina,* and the potent concoction was already snaking through my body, on her way to my stomach and the worlds beyond.

The journey had been a very strong one and had knocked me out until lunchtime the following day. It was hard to make sense of. The only thing I remembered clearly was my encounter and exchange with the spirit of a pretty fern-like plant, whom I had noticed growing next to my hut. Ah, what a sweetie she was! In my journey, I saw her covered in droplets of water, as if she had just been rained on. As water collected at the tips of her leaves, she extended one of them toward me. I stretched my arm out, and the droplet at the tip of the shiny leaf glittered. Hanging from the leaf edge with the same excited tension of a skydiver ready to freefall, the droplet detached, free for a fleetingly moment before landing in the soft center of my cupped hand. "Oryngham," the plant said, as a wave of warmth hit my heart. "This is our word for 'thank you.'" I was confused—why would the plants be thanking me? I felt I should have been the one giving thanks. "Thank you for listening," she continued softly, "for being open to receive our gifts, for meeting us in true communion." She paused for a brief moment, as she wrapped her leafy arms around me. Rocking me like a tiny babe in her deep embrace, she hushed, "Now rest, child, rest—we have much work to do." Her beautiful gesture glowed inside me, reverberating. The inaudible sound of her song, or *icaro*[17]—a calming but peculiar tune made of sounds I could not hear and meanings I could not decipher—resonated inside out, ringing through the temple structure of the *maloka,* where Don M had started humming the plant's sacred song.

Back at the temple of modern science in the university where I work, investigations on the nature of reality are carried out under standardized and controlled conditions, mostly within the sanctity of experimental laboratories. With its quest for a source of intellectual security based on objectivity and materialism, the modern scientific mode of thinking—scientific determinism—has become the accepted procedure for gaining knowledge about the world and a common denominator for Western culture. As a result, the knowledge attained by conventional science is, for the most part, an intellectual enterprise abstracted from the subjective experience of the body, the mind, and the spirit.

As pointed out by ecophilosopher David Abram, the deterministic view of a world mechanically governed by causes and effects is commonly opposed by the spiritual idealism of new age circles, where the ethereal nature of spiritual reality is favored over the down-to-earth nature of matter. Each obsessed with its own mythology—both worldviews upholding the notion of a separation between mind, body, and spirit and both prioritizing one aspect of nature over the other—the possibility of their full integration into unity and interdependence drops quickly out of sight.[18] By juxtaposing the apprentice shaman, wide open to the darkness of a Shipibo *maloka* in a defiant wilderness, with the Western scientist locked under the brightness of fluorescent lights in an off-limits controlled-environment laboratory, nature had found a way to integrate and unify the two worldviews. Guided by the plants, the scientist learned to think out and away from the conventional box that measured current scientific precincts, while the shaman inspired an entirely new vision.

Eighteen months later, this integrated perspective gave birth to the first of a series of scientific studies on plant behavioral ecology, which provided clear experimental evidence for the existence of communication channels between plants beyond those recognized and studied by science up until then.[19] Could plants in my scientific laboratory communicate with each other with sound (like they did in the shamanic temple of the Amazon)? Daring to ask this strange and impermissible question certainly invited waves of mockery in the corridors of academic science; far more important, however, was the possibility of unlocking its revolutionary answer. And the answer did come, whispered by a teeny kernel of corn.

Chapter R

All knowledge is borrowed knowledge.

~ Kernels of Truth ~

Ridiculed, scorned, or deliberately ignored, the truth about anything is quirky and awkward when it first emerges. Germinating at the margins of familiarity, the seeds of truth are anomalous occurrences. Out of context—like invasive weeds that do not belong in the well-established terrains of cultural consensus—these anomalies become especially troublesome when they gather to the point that they can no longer be ignored. Then they pose a serious threat, that of undermining the confidence of the existing field, as their blossoming opens the mind into completely uncharted realities and extraordinary possibilities. Beware—these flowers are not for picking! Each belonging to itself alone, the knowledge they carry can never be taken, only gifted. The knowledge they gift can never be owned, only shared. Respectfully. In the end, all knowledge is only ever borrowed.

Back in the Peruvian jungle, Don M had learned how to diagnose and treat his patients from the knowledge that more than one hundred Amazonian plants had gifted him. He had done his first *dieta* with his grandfather when he was just a boy. After a few *dietas* with various *maestros,* the time had come for him to start dieting alone. During one of these solo *dietas* in the middle of the jungle, the spirits of the plants had called him by name and gifted him with dreams, visions, and, of course, their precious medicine songs *(icaros).* These *icaros* are whistled or sung by the shaman during ceremonial or curative rituals to deliver the required medicine, depending on the needs and conditions of the patients. During my visit, Don M explained that each plant has its own song and its own language to sing it. "Some sing in Shipibo," Don M said, "others sing in Quechua, like Mama Coca—the coca plant." And some sing in "other ways"—and he was able to sing these songs during ceremonies even if the language was unknown to him (or simply other-than-human).

As I had experienced myself, these songs are not metaphors but tangible gestures of a plant's fondness to communicate and relate to the human through kinship. They are a blessing that grants the human person access to the enriching powers of the plant person, an invaluable gift generously entrusted to the heart of the shaman as the keeper of knowledge. And for thousands of years, indigenous healers, witchdoctors, and shamans around the world have been learning the songs of plants as a way of communicating with these other-than-human persons and acknowledging them as the guarantors of human existence, the true philanthropists of the world.[1] A relationship built on this premise can only engender a deep sense of gratitude and humbleness that awakens our role as custodians with a duty of care and respect toward these other beings and the vital knowledge they enrich us with.

Without idealizing them unnecessarily, it is fair to say that many indigenous cultures have maintained strong traditional systems of custodianship over these relationships to safeguard their knowledge and uphold the associated responsibilities for their use.[2] It is quite the opposite in contemporary Western society, where the lack of appreciation for the preciousness of our relationship with these vegetal others has promoted a destructive attitude that fails to recognize both our absolute dependence on these relationships and our obligation to protect, nurture, and care for them. In this state of neglect and disregard, the cultural construction of plants as *objects* becomes an indispensible distortion—wheat, oats, and barley are reduced to slavery as crops on production lines and eucalyptus and pine trees tamed and confined in plantation camps, often far away from home, while the unruliness of a natural rainforest is burned or bulldozed to be deplorably eradicated—to support our utilitarian exploitation and monopolization of these vegetal beings as "resources" and to justify our misappropriation and misuse of the knowledge they have brought to humanity.

At its worst, this disconnection reveals one of the many faces of colonialism: the capitalist agro-scientific psychosis whereby plants are seen as commodities to be taken without sanction and the wealth of traditional knowledge regarding them is used without permission. Illogical and offensive, the first order of business of scientific colonialism—also known as biopiracy or bioprospecting, for a more politically correct designation of the same—is to devalue plants and the traditional knowledge of them. By disregarding both the physical and the spiritual personhood of plants and depreciating the traditional knowledge held by indigenous and local communities about them, the scientific colonizers are busy convincing everyone that whatever product they have to offer is superior—better than the unsubstantiated and fanciful belief system preserved as traditional knowledge and certainly wiser than the spiritual pretexts that that system has concocted to prevent its knowledge claims from being scrutinized according to the Western scientific model. Then, with a satisfied grin of entitlement, the international trade organizations and multinational groups engaged in these colonialist assaults proceed to claim ownership over those who are not for sale, patenting and trademarking those who are not theirs for branding. What if the claims of traditional knowledge were indeed put to the test and these "beliefs" substantiated by a Western scientific model? And, more to the point, would the "truth" emerging at the interface between these two bodies of knowledge have the power to change the notion of ownership to one of custodianship?

In the middle of the Peruvian jungle, the Amazonian plants had spoken to me through numinous dreams and visions, telekinetic conversations and songs. As they had done for millennia, they had taught me of their role in supporting the physical, psycho-emotional, and spiritual growth of humanity at the individual, community, and planetary level. This understanding of plant-human communication is yet to fully breach the fortified walls of academia.

Over the last two decades, however, important insights into our understanding of plant ecology and the behavioral nature of plants have not only confirmed the existence of the wide range of communicative means plants use (at least among themselves and some animals) but also, most excitingly, have indicated that more modalities remain to be revealed.[3] Of course, excitement and curiosity epitomize the original spirit of science, but they do not feature much in the standard view of scientific development. Still holding strong, the conventional perception would have knowledge develop in a linear way; the truth about scientific progress, however, is quite different.

As demonstrated by history[4] and eloquently elaborated by the influential philosopher of science Thomas Kuhn, significant breakthroughs in scientific understanding do not occur by adhering to the restrictive conditions of the existing disciplinary template—progress is not made by steadily adding new truths to old ones (and correcting past errors here and there), with developments occasionally accelerated at the hands of an exceptionally brilliant scientist in charge and, most importantly, ensured by—and in the name of—the scientific method.[5] Breaching out of their rooted darkness, breakthroughs are seeds of nonconformity determined to sprout into the light of freethinking. Anomalous, then, the unruly idea that plants are able to communicate in ways that reside outside the box of what is known had to break through the limitations of existing ideology. And that is just about what this idea did in my laboratory, where three plants—chili, fennel, and basil—had come to whisper the imperceptible and insinuate the unfamiliar from the confinement of the plastic boxes I had built for them for an experiment.

Nowadays, these plants are incorporated into cuisines worldwide, but their aromatic fruits and delicious shoots, together with their medicinal actions, were well known and valued by the ancients in Central America, the Mediterranean basin, and all the way to Africa and Asia. Although separate in their wild origins, fiery chili peppers, sweet fennels, and humble basils all braved a similar history of domestication and widespread commercial cultivation, and now they had ventured inside my lab on a mission together for an altogether different reason. In all his spiciness, it was the chili pepper who posed the zesty question to me—how would you learn of what is presently unknown about our vegetal ways of communicating if you are not looking for it and do not even realize that it may exist? Generously, he had also provided the answer—exclude the known to allow yourself to see what unexpected things might happen. And the unexpected is exactly what happened.

Although the idea that plants communicate has long been controversial and debated, important insights into our understanding of plant ecology have confirmed that plants are capable of processing information about their neighbors, both above and below ground, and of sharing information about the resources available in their surroundings. The mechanisms by which plants communicate all this information are complex. We now know, for example, that plants can share information through touch and mechanical contact induced by gravity, as well as through changes in pressure gradients of various nature. They are also proficient at exchanging information via the transmission and reflection of different wavelengths of light. For example, plants have evolved specific photoreceptors (e.g., phytochrome B) that allow them to monitor specific changes in the level of the far-red relative to the red component of sunlight and thus perceptive neighboring plants, particularly the proximity of future competitors.

Also, the recent literature is replete with studies that show how plants communicate chemically. For example, plants are able to warn each other of approaching insect attacks using an extensive "vocabulary" of chemical molecules, such as herbivore-induced volatile organic compounds.[6] Through this airborne plant-plant communication channel, plants are able to respond to cues produced by injured neighbors when they are not yet attacked or damaged themselves. What if we blocked all of these modalities? Would the plants be still able to respond to each other?

The idea for an experimental box that would allow me to block out all sources of information we then knew plants use in order to recognize and evaluate their neighbors was first conceived on a plane to the Philippines in early 2010. Designed to successively silence layers of expression and meaning, it consisted of a central cylindrical box housed within two different-sized square boxes, which were nested inside one another like Russian matryoshka dolls (Figure 1).

The air in between the two square outer boxes was removed to create a vacuum, a barrier of empty space that besieged all of the plants inside each unit, hence accounting for and blocking any possibility of communication or perhaps interference with adjacent experimental units sharing the growth room. The central cylindrical box was designed to allow not even a molecule of chemical murmuring through its sealed walls or the slightest elbowing to be articulated by the plant sealed inside it. When covered in black plastic, it blocked even the feeblest gesturing of light between the plants.

And so for several months, I followed thousands of chili seeds as they grew into seedlings inside their matryoshka boxes while coexisting with their neighboring plants. Naturally, plant neighbor relationships take several forms, and gardeners have long appreciated that some species engage in unfriendly exchanges, while others like helping each other. In fact, these relationships between plants have been brought into play in both small vegetable gardens as well as large agricultural and silvopastoral plantation systems around the world. Far from being based on anecdotes or folklore, this approach to planting (commonly known as "companion planting") echoes the scientific notion that neighboring species affect one another through negative competitive as well as positive facilitative interactions, a key component of many ecological theories.

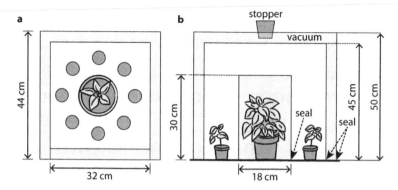

Figure 1. Schematic representation of the custom designed experimental unit (not to scale). (a) The seal at the base of the central cylindrical box ensured that chili seeds arranged in a circle around the adult plant were chemically isolated from it. (b) All seeds and adult plants within a replicate unit were housed within two different-sized square boxes, one inside the other, with the air in between the two boxes removed using a vacuum pump. The whole experimental unit was custom-made in colorless cast-acrylic material (ModenGlas), which transmitted 92 percent of visible light but was opaque to ultraviolet and infrared wavelengths. Figure originally published in: M. Gagliano, M. Renton, N. Duvdevani, M. Timmins, and S. Mancuso, "Out of Sight but Not Out of Mind: Alternative Means of Communication in Plants." PLoS ONE 7, no.5 (2012): e37382.

With this context in mind, I watched the little chilies grow either on their own or in the presence of another plant inside the central box, whether this involved the disturbing interference of fennel, the wholesome companionship of basil, or the familial comfort of an adult chili. Because fennel is known to exude aggressive chemicals that inhibit growth and even kill other plants around him, I expected his presence in the box to retard or block the germination and growth rates of the young chili when open contact was possible; however, I envisaged that this negative effect on germination would become progressively smaller as his signals were partially or totally blocked.

Basil, on the other hand, is well known as the ideal companion to chili plants by virtue of his ability to keep the soil moist and act as organic living mulch (as well as being an effective natural insecticide and inhibiting the germination and root growth of common competitive weeds). Accordingly, I expected his presence in the box to enhance the germination rates of chili seeds, both when open contact and light signaling was allowed; however, I expected there to be no particularly positive effect when all known signals were totally blocked.

Some of my expectations proved to be spot on, while others were surprisingly off the mark. I found that germination rates were distinctly low when the seeds were grown on their own, but even lower when openly exposed to the volatile chemicals of the notoriously inimical fennel—no surprises there. What was unanticipated was the fact that the young chili accelerated their germination rates when the fennel was present but its signals were partially or totally blocked. This intriguing finding demonstrated that the young plants were able to recognize the potential for the interfering presence of their bad neighbor and swiftly respond to their situation by adjusting their growth. As expected, germination rates improved with other chili plants around and, unsurprisingly, were even better in the benevolent presence of basil. This finding clearly validated the claims of many gardeners who recognize the beneficial effect of basil on the growth of chili plants. To me, however, the exciting finding was that this effect was true even when all known signals from the basil were blocked. In other words, the supportive interaction observed between these two species was mediated via a signaling modality other than those studied thus far (light, chemicals, and touch).

What emerged was clear and scientifically defendable—with the guidance of the plants, I had uncovered a previously undocumented communication channel. The young chili plants knew of the presence and identity of their neighboring plant (whether a good or bad companion), even when light signals, airborne chemicals, root contact, and possible shared fungal networks were all blocked. The question was, *how* did they know?

There are plenty of good ecological reasons why young plants would need to be aware of their neighbors. Often on a shoestring energy budget, plants can have a hard time dividing their limited resources in growth and defense simultaneously. Therefore, when it comes to friends and relatives, plants may facilitate one another by engaging in cooperative and altruistic behaviors. However, when competitive interactions are unavoidable, the perception of any signal that heralds the advent of a competitor before any actual shortage of resources takes place would be beneficial, allowing young plants to adjust their shape and growth in response to the presence of a competitor or even a possible aggressor.

So considered from the perspective of a young chili pepper, there was clearly nothing sweet about a neighboring fennel, who is infamous for suppressing germination and growth of other plants by releasing chemicals. But how was it possible that the presence of a fennel who could not be seen, smelled, or touched was sufficient for the chili seeds to hurry their germination and for seedlings to change their growth trajectory? Also, seedlings grew differently depending on whether the neighbor was a fennel or an adult chili (Figure 2); once again, the question was, how did they know who was growing next to them when such neighbor was supposed to be undetectable? They knew. And they also knew that despite millennia of domestication, their seeds remained wild at heart and were rupturing the rock-solid layers of cultivated science.

By probing into the mindscape of the unimagined, this initial experimental work had started unveiling the topographies of an unexplored reality. How exhilarating to discover the existence of uncharted communication channels used by seeds and seedlings to sense neighbors and identify relatives. The fact that there was no mechanistic explanation for *how* plants performed these feats provided the intriguing touch of mystery and suspense that made the resultant scientific papers absorbing (to write and read), similar to a good detective novel.[7] And this was the very thing that ruffled the academic establishment: what was the mechanism that explained my results? For, surely, without an explanation of how they did it, it simply couldn't be!

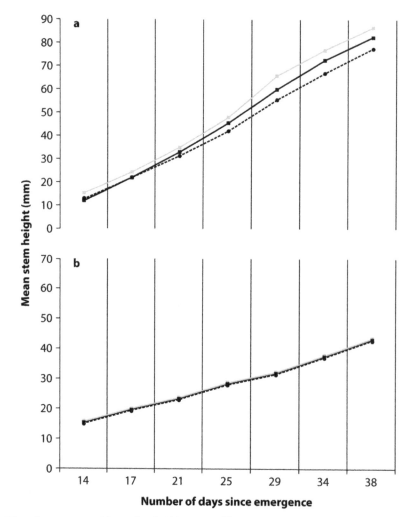

Figure 2. Early growth of chili seedlings depends on the presence and identity of their neighbor. (a) Seedlings growing next to a fennel (grey solid line and triangles) are marginally taller than those growing next to an adult chili plant (black solid line and squares) and significantly taller than seedlings in the empty control (black dotted line and white diamonds). The observed differences in above-ground growth among treatments (adult

fennel plant, grey solid line and triangles; adult chili plant, black solid line and squares; empty control, black dotted line and white diamonds) are amplified over time. (b) Growth differences disappear when seedlings are allowed to grow in the absence of any adult plant after emergence. Figure originally published in: M. Gagliano, M. Renton, N. Duvdevani, M. Timmins, and S. Mancuso, "Out of Sight but Not Out of Mind: Alternative Means of Communication in Plants." PLoS ONE 7, no.5 (2012): e37382.

During the peer-review process of this work, it was pointed out that the approach used was not the way scientific research is normally carried out. There is usually an idea that a particular factor could significantly affect a process under consideration, and the experiment is designed to prove the significance of this factor. To allow for the unexpected to happen with no preconception about what one is even looking for seemed unorthodox, and it was this unorthodoxy that was perceived as an infringement of the conventional touchstone for scientific legitimacy. And in a sense, the approach was transgressive indeed—irritatingly free of actual methodological, analytical, or other technical faults, it was violating the ontological[8] boundaries of a science made for humans and exclusively by humans. By allowing for any pattern to emerge rather than constraining the view of what one should expect to see, this initial research was a collaborative effort with my plant associates, one that activated the process of unbinding both the plant and the human from what was considered permissible within the prevailing scientific belief system. It was in the salubrity of this garden-fresh soil that one of the three sisters[9]—the sacred corn plant (maize)—raised her voice and wanted in on the action, as we shall see.

In the midst of the rich symphony of nature, plants appear utterly silent.[10] Because we are designed to believe our own perceptions, our human experience of their silence is so obvious and undeniable that we forget to question whether plants truly are as voiceless as we perceive them. Admittedly, without offering some proof of plant voice—assuming we agreed on the definition of *voice*[11]—we may rightly deem the question itself to be nonsense. However, to forget to ask the question, in effect, dismisses any chance for the proof to emerge. As a matter of fact, this is exactly what colonial ideologies of domination and manipulation have succeeded at; by scorning traditional knowledge as unsubstantiated and fanciful and erasing our ancestral memories that spoke of other possibilities, humanity has found itself locked inside the experimental box of a restraining sociocultural view.

Like the plants in my experimental matryoshka boxes, we are besieged by a barrier of emptiness designed to block any possibility of communication. From this viewpoint, of course, plants do not speak! The good news is that by simply asking the question regarding vegetal speech, we are free to move away from the self-righteous slumber we have numbed our mind with. By merely asking the question about plant voice, we set ourselves free from the preconceived notion that construes plants as inevitably voiceless, and we open ourselves to observing plants as they actually behave and to discovering the reality we share. That's right, because voice is an *inter* -subjective affair. Voice exists in the place of relation, the space between the self and the other, and it is what we bring to our encounters with plants that defines the quality of our communicative rendezvous—those we allow to speak (or those we silence).[12]

If there truly is a plant voice, how does it speak? How can we hear it? The voice of the vegetal other is revealed in a place of reciprocity. At this point, some would argue that our dialogue with plants lacks reciprocity, as it would seem that for plants to do the talking, we are required merely to be the listeners (never the speakers). This argument would be based on the recognition that dialogue entails a mutual exchange, in which the one who speaks must be also able to hear, and the one who hears is also capable of speaking. Accordingly, it would be concluded that there is no dialogue at all between plants and us, because we are supposed to give them our full attention, but they never engage with and respond to us.[13] In the course of my research, this perception was about to be, if not completely debunked, severely altered by a new scientific truth.

As in all conversations, the relationship between how information is packaged (encoding) and the content translated (decoding) determines the outcome of the exchange and interaction. The experimental findings from my matryoshka boxes had provided no mechanistic explanation of how the chili seedlings exchanged information with the other plants, but they had signposted the way. It was clear that some of the underlying conditions required for such conversation to occur included the emission of a signal that not only conveyed real-time information about neighboring plants but also could be analyzed quickly by the receiving seedlings. And what better way to have a chat than thru sound?[14] After all, the ability to sense sound and vibrations is behind the behavioral organization of all living organisms and their relationship with their environment. It was in late 2011 that bright yellow kernels of corn decided to break the silence with their vibratory signals. Their conversation sprouted inside a university laboratory in Bristol, England—at the heart of one of the leading global colonial powers—and for the first time, their loud and chirpy vegetal clicks were heard by our ears and recorded by our sensitive scientific laser instruments. And it was official—plants emit sounds, they hear them, and on the basis of what they hear, they modify their behavior.[15]

Emerging at the interface between two bodies of knowledge, the truth was that this research was successfully substantiating the "beliefs" of traditional knowledge through the application of the Western scientific model. Did it succeed in changing the notion of ownership to one of custodianship? By raising her voice, corn had done something more, something different. Beautifully unexpected—like a rare flower blossoming out of season—her voice had brought into awareness a new perceptual field extending beyond ownership *and* custodianship, a vision of nonhierarchical co-participation. By revealing the vegetal voice, corn had come to ask that we recognize our attempts at silencing plants, because humans have something of a track record for silencing those whose voice they do not want to hear. We do this by unconsciously ignoring them or deliberately stripping them away,[16] and this is an injurious act because it violates the very thing that makes dialogue possible—the recognition of the other as an equal.

From this perspective, both ownership and custodianship break down the foundation of a true dialogue with the vegetal. Although the two attitudes are different, both are validated by the apparent inability of plants to express themselves, which creates a justification for objectifying them. Denying the morally relevant value of the interaction, ownership is designed to override the subjectivity of plants in order to control and abuse with no restrain. On the other hand, custodianship inadvertently patronizes them by treating them with a kindness that gives away our feeling of superiority. This attitude is most obviously observed (although, rarely understood for what it truly accomplishes) when we overwrite plants with the sounds that are familiar to us by ventriloquizing them through the approximation of human speech[17] or the transposition of musical scales and various instruments onto them.[18]

In dialogue with the plant world, we are asked to relinquish these built-in ideas that make our perspective better than, wiser than, and superior to the other, all these attitudes bring us to the same ethical and moral cul-de-sac. And with a few chirpy sounds, corn had effortlessly brought it all to the surface for us to honestly view it, if willing. Personally, I had always considered myself as a custodian of the vegetal world and, more generally, of nature, but seeing myself as a steward above and separate from the rest was a position no longer tenable. In opening the conversation, corn had delivered a transformative message—plants and nature can be heard. They are not property to be owned. They need not custodianship, but a commitment to a nonhierarchical respect, a space of communion in which we come to understand the world and take the pathway toward understanding each other.

And this was only the beginning.

Chapter Y

You are not looking for answers; all answers are already here. You are looking for the questions; know your questions, and you will see the answers.

~ The Bear's Cauldron ~

Yardsticks uphold our judgments by measuring our common sense of reality. Sensibly positioned at the verge of the real, these edge markers stand proud in all their calculated brilliance. There, they ensure a traveler's safety by guiding a life's journey along the well-beaten path. Sentinels to our inner movements, they crown our minds and chain our hearts. And as a reward for our compliance, they keep us unquestioning within the tranquil confines of well-attended green lawns, bejeweled by the picture-perfect white picket fences of modern suburbia. All the while, off all beaten paths and beyond all fences, the wild answers of tall, rowdy grasses and boisterous weeds enliven the unruly ground of the unknown; with their dazzling colors and perfumed blossoms, these answers keep inviting questions to come and find them. The answer is there before we have a chance to ask what is there; it is the answer that beckons us to it, not the question. So if you catch yourself wondering whether you would stray off the path or jump that fence to follow your answer, know that you have been invited to dare.

It was a hot summer afternoon in suburbia. My friends Sa and Claudio were packing up their things, ready to move to their new home up in the hills. At times like these, vans are particularly useful, as they ease you into your newfound role as the moving champion while keeping your stress levels in check. I happened to have one, and I had driven it over to help with the move. In the midst of boxes chockablock with books, a Japanese wooden table in one corner, and the washing machine in another, Sa appeared with two cold drinks, sat me down, and started telling me about her latest trip to Queensland. She had been invited to a gathering of grandmothers—indigenous elders, medicine women, and spiritual leaders from various lineages—and, of course, I was all ears as she shared her impressions of the experience and the incredible women she met there. Converging on the East Coast of Australia from various places around the globe, each grandmother had a powerful presence, which brought something special to the gathering, and now Sa was weaving their uniqueness with the invisible threads of her voice and bringing to life one grandmother at the time, each presence filling a house being emptied. I was completely captivated by her stories.

Sa abruptly stood up, excited. She briefly disappeared from the room and returned with a small leather pouch and a mysterious round tin, shining in her hands. "Try, try this!" she said as she opened the silvery lid. "I know this, but can't quite place it," I uttered, as the strong scent of the fine brown powder inside the little tin wandered off through a maze of memories, where it could not find home. Before I could think, my little finger had already dipped into the powder and dispensed it to my tongue. "Mmm, I know this..." I said slowly, as the spicy flavor of the powder delivered a burst of simple knowing, one that my brain was racing to decipher. "But what is it?" I asked. "It is called osha," she said, and as she pulled something dark brown and kind of hairy out of the small pouch, she added, "and this is what the root looks like before it gets powdered." She sipped at her drink before continuing. "A Native American grandmother gave it to me, mentioning that someone would come for it and that I would know when. Well ... I think this root is for you."

That night, I nibbled at the osha root before going to bed. And I dreamed. I dreamed of a luxurious rich brown. It was dark brown everywhere I felt, and its warmth enveloped me completely. Its wild motion tossed me uncontrollably this way and that. With both hands, I was holding on to its softness with the commitment of a flea on the back of a gargantuan animal. Then it occurred to me—that was exactly where I was! I was riding on the back of some enormous, furry wild animal as it ran who knows where. And with that realization, the dream ended, but the vivid kinesthetic feeling of it stayed with me till morning. What was that? Did it have anything to do with the osha root? Somehow I knew it did, although I had no idea how I knew. I also knew that the dream was only the beginning of something, although I had no idea of what that something was or what was to come next. So I decided to find out. And what better way to take matters into one's own hands than by beating a drum?

During the week following my peculiar dream, I used the repetitive drumming of a large hoop drum to bring myself into an altered state of perception with the idea of learning more about the osha root, my dream, and—perhaps—the connection between the two, if any was to be found. While drumming is part of an old shamanic practice, I had learned of it only a few years earlier, when I had found myself at a drum-making workshop and had started experiencing the hypnotic and truly mind-altering effects of shamanic drumming.[1] Now, the thunderous voice of my drum carried me to the verge of ordinary reality; from there, its powerful beat pushed me over the threshold and into the unseen underside of reality, in a search for the question that would reveal the answer that had called me. And this is how we first met face-to-face.

Absorbed within the driving pulse of my drum, I found myself holding onto the marvelous rich brown fur of her back, just as I had done in my dream. *She* was a bear—a staggeringly oversized brown bear, to be precise. Full of purpose, she was running somewhere into a forest, carrying me on her back. Once at the destination she had intended to reach, she came to a halt, which, to my great relief, also meant the end of my wild roller-coaster ride. No longer on her back, I was now standing with my feet on the ground. I was teeny-weeny, and there was a certain elven look about me, which I found intriguing. I was absorbed, staring right up an extremely large black tunnel, the nostril of what possibly was the most refined nose in the animal kingdom. The bear's huge nose was inspecting the tiny human form standing in front of her, and all the while, the air moving in and out of her nostrils was gusting warmly on my face. Heavily built, her disproportionally large body was bent down low over me as I stared, spellbound and unable to move.

A brilliant shaft of light filtering from above and faraway penetrated the thick darkness of the forest that surrounded us. In that juxtaposition of light and darkness, the bear appeared even more enormous, towering over me in all her might. Was she going to kill me any minute now? As if acknowledging my thought, she opened her massive mouth, sporting an impressive collection of large pearlies. Then, without uttering a word, she said, "Of course, I could kill you if I wanted to. But I won't." And with that, she sat down on the ground. I mirrored her and sat down too. We looked at each other, and I asked why she had come to meet me. Was there something she wanted me to know? Uttering no words, she said, "Come back every day for your training. I assure you that I am already working on you." At that point, the rhythm of my drumbeat changed of its own accord. The bridge created by its roaring sound faded, and I was back in this reality.

The next day, I felt a strong call to journey again. The feeling was one of commitment and urgency, as if I had signed up to attend an important class at some Earth-like school in an invisible dimension, and I couldn't be late. The monotonous rhythm of the drum delivered me straight to the patch of dense forest I had visited the previous day. There the miniature me sat once again in front of the oversized bear. At once, I knew—she was Osha. Both eager and wary, I asked without a sound, "What are we doing here?" Osha explained matter-of-factly, "You are getting ready—and I am preparing you—for the real teaching to take place."

I was listening as if I understood what she had conveyed, but I really had no clue. What teaching was she referring to? And what did "getting ready" mean? But before I could get lost in reveries, she said (wordlessly), "Lesson number one." Then, with a commanding tone, "Sit up straight and center yourself." I did what she instructed at once. And as I did, I started growing. Like a young plant would, the little me was now visibly growing toward the brilliant beam of light I had noticed during my previous visit. All of a sudden, I realized I was going to grow as big as the bear. And as quickly as that realization entered my awareness, I was small again, with the brilliant light washing over my head as it filtered thru the trees from faraway, piercing the darkness that surrounded us.

Puzzled and disoriented, I looked up at the bear still sitting in front of me, who was now gently patting the top of my head in a motherly fashion. "Before you grow like that, you must prepare," she explained. I had no time to ask how one prepares, as she continued with a kind and firm tone, "Sit quietly in the darkness of your soul. There is no fear. It is the darkness that contains all the potential to become light."

The next thing I knew was that I was buried in the ground—yes, *planted* in the soil, like a seed, a seed of potential. I knew then that before growth, I had to sit in the darkness that resides under the surface. Unafraid, I asked Osha what was she going to do with me now. In a tender gesture of her brown paw, she said, "Fertilizing, enriching the soil with the nutrients required for the plant coming out of the seed to be strong." Then she inhaled deeply, and with profound conviction, she added, "It needs to be strong."

Several other meetings with Osha followed. We would meet in the same dark patch of forest, sit in front of one another, and "talk." This is how she would deliver her lessons to me. Then, during one of these meetings, *that* side of reality became practically relevant to *this* side, where things were waiting to be actualized (although I didn't know that at the time). So as the sound of my drum boomed through the silence once more, I was back there. This time I saw a huge cauldron sitting on an open fire roaring between us. Osha was holding a large wooden stick and stirring the bubbling contents of the pot. Silently humming a kind of lullaby, the big bear seemed so completely engrossed in her cooking activities that one could be forgiven for thinking that she had not noticed my presence. I was stretching this way and that in a futile attempt to get a glimpse of what was cooking, but I was simply too small to see anything at all. "What are you cooking in that cauldron?" my tiny self uttered soundlessly. As she kept her absolute focus on the boiling contents, a grin appeared on her bear face. "I am cooking your medicine, of course. It is almost ready." And I found myself back in the room, holding my drum.

"Does any of this make sense to you?" I asked Sa one afternoon, as I finished recounting my drumming escapades and pedagogical meetings with Osha in the dark forest that extended beyond the enclosure of picketed reality. Sa smiled, delighted. "Oh, I forgot to tell you. Osha root is also known as 'bear root' or 'bear medicine.'"[2] Within, I felt my body tremble in shock and excitement. Panic-stricken, my mind scurried through its archive of orderly knowledge and logical explanations in a frantic attempt to find a sensible way out of the disquieting situation at hand. And as my mind, all jumbled up, came to the conclusion *It makes no sense,* my voice announced with confidence, "Now, that makes perfect sense!" *What?* my mind thought, *It doesn't make any sense whatsoever!* But before I had time to grasp the absurdity of the whole situation, I heard myself saying, "I knew I had met the spirit of the plant. She has been cooking medicine for me and preparing me for something that lies ahead." And in a sober tone, I continued, "It is time for me to contact the Native American grandmother who gave you this root."

My first contact with her was by email. I introduced myself, mentioning my strong dreams and visions of red pipes, plant roots, and bears. I had no doubt that I was to travel to visit her, and I said as much. I also had no doubt that a vision was waiting for me in Bear Country, and I said that much too. I was aware that my words were a little blunt and perhaps even odd for a first contact. I was taking the risk of being disregarded as kind of kooky, but how else could I express the loud call I had heard? A few days later, I received a response: "Hi Monica, I am happy to hear from you and that you are listening to the voice of the spirits! Yes, indeed, it sounds like it is time to go pray on the hill, doing a vision quest." The email provided the necessary information regarding appropriate preparation, as well as details on the Lakota protocols for the vision quest ceremony, which was to be held in May in the California mountains. The email finished with "many blessings, and thank you for listening to your ancestors" and was signed by Mato Ta Pejuta Wakan Najin. Her name means Bear Medicine Standing Sacred.

All this happened in late January 2012. This can be a nerve-wracking part of the year if you work at an Australian university. It is our time for writing bids for the big honeypot of federal funding, a limited number of grants and fellowships from the Australian Research Council, which not only awards money for our research but also, in many cases, covers our salaries. Our grant craftsmanship is put to a serious test because of the added pressure that failure to secure such funding can result in the termination of an academic career. This was where I stood. The fast-approaching end of my existing fellowship was suspended over my neck like the blade of a guillotine, and the odds were that the blade would come down, delivering, with its notorious efficacy, the fatal promise. During this period, I experienced several bouts of profound anxiety accompanied by a deep sorrow for the possible loss. Scared, I was frantically flapping my wings, trying to escape the chilling whispers of a hopelessness that wanted to consume me.

Years later, I would learn what my experience of emotions like anxiety was really about and how to harness these emotions' gifts—yes, gifts. Anxiety, for example, is a valuable messenger, one that speaks of my prevailing belief construct and its sphere of influence. This belief construct is like a container, which I take to be objective reality, and anxiety always arises to alert me when I have reached the edge of the container. Anxiety speaks of the uneasiness of staying within the container's fortified walls once their restrictive presence is felt, and in this rests its precious gift—the call to break down the walls of personalized assumptions and outgrown perspectives, the invitation to realize new possibilities, when my current restricted understanding sees only impossibilities. This is why coping with anxiety does not really stop the anxiety; the answer is not in understanding and resolving anxiety, but in changing perspective so that anxiety simply disappears. When it happens, the precious gift it brings is one of joy and excitement for life. Back then, however, I had no appreciation of this, so I simply tried to cope.

To remedy my situation, I would get to work early in the morning, but instead of going straight to my office, I would sit on the grass under one of the eucalyptus trees that stood tall along the river's edge. Sipping my coffee, I would stare at the sunlight as it poured over the surface of the water and flickered here and there with a kind of restless aliveness. At times, the sunlit surface would have a liquid calmness about it; then, as by some kind of magic, it would be persuaded into a dance of familiar lines, a fluid movement drawn by the appearance and disappearance of a pod of glossy fins, irregular triangular silhouettes decorated by personalized markings, the living scars of existence. At other times, two large black swans would appear in their dark outfits, wearing white lipstick on beaks the color of blood. Suddenly, one long neck would plunge underwater, and all was left for the eyes to see was a raft of feathers floating on the surface. As a child who knows what will happen next but nevertheless waits with gleeful excitement, I would wait for the moment the graceful neck would reappear, often with a chance piece of weed still hanging off its beak. I would watch the pair as they passed by, appearing nonchalant, while concealed from view, strong red feet were swiftly paddling them on.

These were moments of an inspired ... *something,* a something that would percolate from the roots under my feet, rising up to bring the fresh breeze of self-assurance to my heart. No longer flapping hysterically, but uplifted by a sense of deep courage,

I would open my wings wide and, keeping them extended, as eagles do, I would catch my inner updraft and circle high in the sky of my mind. From that perspective, I could not see what the future held, but I could see what the present called for. I answered.

The research officer said, "Monica, that is career suicide!" in response to my decision to write a proposal on understanding sound communication in plants for the upcoming round of grant applications from the Australian Research Council. The university had organized a series of workshops to assist researchers like me in the preparation and writing of their applications. In one of the first workshops, applicants from a wide range of disciplines had been asked to put together a succinct, one-paragraph summary, pitched in such manner that would be comprehensible to people who weren't specialists in the field. Each participant would read his or her summary to the group, which would then provide feedback and constructive comments.

When my turn came, I was met with a scornful "Is this a joke? That is not science!" from a colleague sitting a few chairs away from me. With his condescending arrogance, he expressed his mockery blatantly, but I knew he was not alone in feeling that way. In fact, many felt the same, but they preferred to stay silent, maintaining the appearance of decorous collegial behavior, without realizing that their silence spoke volumes. For over two years, for example, a colleague in my own department had looked past me as we passed in the corridors, as though I were transparent—he had decided never to respond to my "hello" or "how you doin'" as a form of prophylaxis, just in case my research ideas on plants turned out to be virulent maladies that could infect his mind and, by mere association, irreversibly taint his career.

Because of such experiences, I was acutely aware of the high-risk nature of my proposal. It was true, as the research officer had pointed out on several occasions, that applying for funding to conduct research in the area of coral reef fishes ecology, where I had a strong and competitive track record, was a much safer approach, because the whole research field was well established, a known quantity. But for me, the question of whether to jump or not to jump the fence of safety and the known had long been off my list of considerations—I was already walking the unbeaten path in response to the wild answers that were calling me. Hence, I wrote my plant bioacoustics proposal, submitted it in March, and waited for the outcome to be announced the next November.

Jetlagged, I walked outside the arrivals terminal of San Francisco International Airport, where a black SUV and a friendly young woman were waiting to meet me. The woman had not only come to scoop me up from the airport—but as I was about to learn, she was also going to host me at her house for the next few days while I gathered all supplies and finalized the preparations for the forthcoming vision quest ceremony. These few days included my first meeting with Mato Ta Pejuta Wakan Najin, to whom I offered tobacco wrapped in red cloth and respectfully made my official request for her guidance and blessing. At this occasion, I also met my "supporter," an older woman who had generously pledged to assist me in preparing for the quest; she had sewn me a lovely ceremonial dress the color of grass and procured for me a pair of hand-stitched moccasins. Later she would source beautiful bunches of white sage as offerings and would eat, drink, pray, and sing for me while I was on my quest. She would also take her turn preparing food for the group at the camp, as well as help organizing the wood for the sacred fire, looking after the fire keeper, and offering fluids to Mato Ta Pejuta Wakan Najin, who would be fasting and holding a safe container for this profound ceremony.

And so, before long, there we were, a convoy of fifteen to twenty people driving several hours north to a private property in the mountains, a wilderness preserve with no phones, toilets, electricity, or drinking water. This would be home to all of us for a few days. Here, the Hanbleche yapi (vision quest) ceremony would take place, and no one was to leave the site once the ceremony started.

While the supporters and helpers set up our basecamp, Mato Ta Pejuta Wakan Najin showed me a few potential sites for my quest. The sites we visited were lush and covered in flowers, but we both agreed that none of them seemed to truly call me. We drove farther up the mountain. We stopped the car where the path ended, walked a little farther up, and there it was! The site was a clearing at the top of the mountain next to a huge oak tree, and this time there was no hesitation. As Mato Ta Pejuta Wakan Najin and I returned to basecamp, her assistants marked a small spot with four willow poles planted at the cardinal points—north, south, east, and west—each one tied with a sacred tobacco flag. They used the prayer ties I had prepared the previous day to create a sacred altar within this spot, a circle inside which I would stay during my vision quest. Inside the altar, they placed a forked willow pole holding a sacred flag with an eagle feather attached to a shell; inside the flag, there was tobacco, spirit food, and a special medicine from Mato Ta Pejuta Wakan Najin's altar, which would protect me and bring visions during my journey.

The Hanbleche yapi is an important rite of passage that offers clarity into the next phase of life. This is exactly what I would find, but I didn't know that yet. I didn't know that the most incredible circumstances were whispering from the distance of space, waiting to meet me. I didn't know that life was pregnant with enchantment, and I had been planted as its timeless emanation. And, most importantly, I didn't know that the whole process would take several years to unfold, but it would and without fail. I certainly had no idea that its essence would wait on the perfect time and eventually pour itself into the pages of a book—*this* book. All I knew then was that I was excited about "going to the mountain" to seek my vision—a time to leave everyone and everything behind and go off alone in nature with my plea to be shown how to be of service to this planet and the greater good. And so the time had come. I gave thanks to the sacred fire, which was to burn continuously during the ceremony and thus required helpers to attend to it twenty-four hours a day. Wearing my ceremonial dress and moccasins and carrying my sacred pipe, I stepped inside the *inipi* (sweat lodge) for the "dust-off," in which Mato Ta Pejuta Wakan Najin purified me to prepare me for my journey to the spirit world. As I walked out of the lodge, all of the helpers were standing with their backs turned, as protocol demanded; nobody was to look at or talk to me until my return from the mountain and only after a second dust-off lodge, which would bring me back from the spirit world and safely re-ground me in this one. My vision was blurred, and my perception felt altered. I realized I had formally departed. Unsteady on my feet, I held my gaze low to the ground while I was accompanied to the car and taken to my altar, where I would stay alone, without food or water, for the following four days.

Inside my sacred circle, which was just large enough for me to lie down in, I flickered in and out of this world. Back flat on the raw ground, I shivered in the cold of the nocturnal air and thanked the sky for not pouring its rain over me. As Mato Ta Pejuta Wakan

Najin had instructed me, I tried to stay awake at night, when the spirit world was more likely to visit. So I stared at the stars wheeling overhead and waited for a time that felt, at once, long and short. Visitors came and went; some were familiar acquaintances, and others were new. I had no fear; my spirit was calm, my body very cold. And that is why, when the first rays of morning light pierced the mantle of the night and released me from the vigil, I felt a premature sense of respite that the sun had come to warm my bones. The relief was indeed premature, because I was soon to discover that in spite of its proximity, the canopy of the huge oak tree branching out next to me provided no shade to my circle. As the hours passed by and the sun moved higher and higher across the crystal clear sky, my skin started burning under the radiant heat, and the tantalizing shade of the mighty tree was transformed into a torturous yearning.

In the raw wilderness of nature and the weakness of fasting, I kept floating between the dreamy waters of my inner world and the surrounding sounds and colors of the outer. Then, suddenly, my attention stirred away from the stinging pain of boredom and sunburned skin to a subtle rustle moving in the forest behind me. There was no need to look to see who was there; I knew. I glimpsed the luxurious rich brown I had seen in my dreams months earlier. My body was still; I felt strangely calm, and as she had said during my first lesson with her, there was no fear.

She had called me here from far away, and I had answered her call. In her cauldron, she had been cooking the medicine for my soul, and now she had come to honor my presence in person. She knew perfectly who I was and what I was doing there, and likewise, I knew her and was confident she hadn't come to hurt me. It was only a brief greeting, a moment for acknowledging one another, and then, as quietly as she had arrived, she vanished back in the darkness of the forest. Later, upon my return to basecamp, I would be told that a large female brown bear had been spotted coming down from the vicinity of my site and had visited basecamp.

At the top of my mountain, time played wiles as a skilled negotiator. I was no longer aware of how many days I had been there or how much time I had left before having to come down. A sense of anxiety started creeping in, and the dragon of doubt started spitting its fire—a fire fiercer than the sun on my skin. Would my prayer be answered? What if I hadn't been heard? What if I had done something wrong? Was I failing? Maybe I hadn't prayed hard enough, long enough, right enough—maybe I was not good enough.

I was bearing witness to my own undoing when the oak tree spoke. "Tell our stories," he stated with authority. Startled, I looked up toward the old tree. He reiterated, "You are here to tell our stories." And the conversation began. If I had had pen and paper (which, of course, I did not), I could have written down a list of all the things that, according to the tree, I was here to do. I was fumbling around inside my mind, as he, endlessly calm and steady, went on emphasizing how important my scientific work was as a medium for the plant people. I would tell their stories, which would reveal them—the plant people—to the human mind and, in so doing, would deliver something humanity urgently needed to feel. Then, suddenly, I was there with him, truly listening, as he said, "There is a lot of traveling ahead of you, and many elders around the world are waiting for you to arrive." I waited for him to pause. I felt overwhelmed by the enormity of what he was describing, as a second dragon—the dragon of self-pity—stomped its way in. "It all sounds amazing, but it is easy for you to speak—all well and good for you, who are rooted in the ground where you are provided with everything you need," I said. "In my world of humans, I need money to do all the things you are asking me to do, and without a job, how can I deliver the science you are talking about?"

I spoke with a lamenting tone to justify my position. I felt a sense of hopelessness. I feared that my prayer had been heard and answered, but I was not going to be able to fulfill it. How could I do all this scientific work and travel to all these places, which were apparently waiting for me, when I was about to lose my academic job and would have no money to even support myself? My questions were unspoken, but the tree heard them all the same. He shuddered his leaves, as if a breeze had come out of nowhere to move them, and replied, "You need not worry about those boring details. We are well aware of your needs, and every single one of them has already been taken care of." I didn't understand, and the old tree seemed totally disinterested in explaining any further.

I assumed our conversation was over, but I was wrong. Still, I looked away, took a deep breath, and with it, I took in the whole view. It was magnificent! I was sitting at the top of a mountain, as close to the turquoise sky as I could be. Two bald eagles were swooping through the air at an incredible speed, doing the most spectacular tricks as they plunged down into the valley below and then hitchhiked a ride up on a thermal to pass me at eye level. With their wings spread wide open, they looked as if they were floating effortlessly. As I watched them, I started feeling their lightness in my own body, and for a moment, I too was gliding with ease, looking down at the deep velvet of the untouched coniferous forest that dressed the sides of the mountainous range all around me. As though I had temporarily acquired the notoriously sharp eyesight of those eagles—possibly the most powerful pair of eyes in the animal kingdom—my own eyes were able to pick up fine details in my field of green and then magnify them with a power four to eight times that of my normal eyesight. I could see the whole forest—each tree as well as the tiniest of grasses growing next to me. And as I acknowledged their individual presence, they all chimed loudly in unison, "Tell our stories! Tell our stories!"

The hardest thing of the whole ceremony was leaving my place of vision. However, upon my return to basecamp, where the sacred fire had never stopped burning and the group had been praying continually and was now waiting for me, I understood that the gifts I had received through my quest belonged to everyone and the world, which really needed it. As Osha had told me months earlier, the little seed of potential that I was needed to grow into a strong presence, one with the courage to do what the world needs. I knew then that her medicine was one of determination and perseverance, nutrients that provided the sustenance for me to embody and give life to the vision I had been given.

My head was still downcast as I returned to the sacred fire and then reentered the lodge for the second dust-off to ground me back into this world. Once I emerged from the *inipi,* a deep sense of joy and gratitude washed over me. It was time for celebration, with a grand feast, as part of the giveaway ceremony—the giving of gifts in thanksgiving. I placed my giveaway on a blanket, and when it was my time, I offered a prayer of thanksgiving to the medicine person, helpers, supporters, and other guests. I was standing next to Mato Ta Pejuta Wakan Najin, and one of the elders who had come to pray approached. He faced Mato Ta Pejuta Wakan Najin and said, "There is great power in this one," and then he turned toward me and, pointing at my heart, said, "You have strong power in you, and you will do great things." His words traveled right to my core, and I thanked him. I knew I had been *seen.*

On my return to Australia, I stopped over in Sydney for a few days to visit my friend Chiara, who is kind of a younger spirit sister, before heading west back to Perth. Chiara and I have known each other for a long time, as we grew up only a few kilometers apart in the north of Italy, where together we had dreamed of migrating to Australia—something we eventually did, albeit ending up in different cities. Whenever possible, I stopped and visited her as I passed through Sydney, and this was one of those occasions. Chiara worked for a major Australian radio and television network, and at the time of my visit, she was carrying out interviews with some remarkable international scholars, thinkers, and activists. They included prominent Aboriginal Australian elders like Uncle B, whom Chiara was meeting for an interview on the day I was returning to Perth. A strange buzz swirled around us as I described to Chiara the instructions I had been given by the plants during my vision quest. Before I knew it, the words spoken by the oak tree were taking material form, and a few days later, I was in Perth having coffee and eating strawberries with Uncle B. By the time August came around, I had been invited to visit him at his home in Mutitjulu, an Aboriginal community at Uluru in the heart of Australia. But that is a story for later.

It was early morning, November 5, 2012. I remember the date very well because my existing fellowship finished on that day. On campus earlier than the usual working hours, I had come to pack my office. My laptop was open on my desk as books of many colors and sizes started coming off the shelf that had been their home for the previous few years. Some landed in a box that I planned to take home; others were assigned to the giveaway pile. Several pieces of experimental equipment came out of hiding in the cupboard where I stored them when they were not in use. In their different shapes and kinds, including some I had custom-built to suit the needs of my research, they looked weird and beautiful—they were the creative tools of a trade designed to explore and reimagine the world. My throat tightened, and the profound anxiety that had silently accompanied me for the whole year was unleashed in all its ferocity.

Then the familiar sound of an incoming email drew my attention to my computer screen. It was from a friend and colleague in Canberra, which, by virtue of being in Australian Eastern Daylight Time, was three hours ahead of Perth—the working day that had not yet started for me was in full swing on the other side of the country. I read the email twice and responded curtly, "Nice joke! Not in the mood ... packing the office." My friend replied with just one line: "Here is the link—check it yourself." My throat tightened even harder, because now my heart was throbbing in it. I clicked on the link and searched for my surname—and there it was, on the Australian Research Council funding announcement webpage. In total disbelief, my shaking hands typed, "Holy shit, I got it!" in my reply to my friend. I had just been awarded a three-year research fellowship for my plant research. I looked out my office window, and there they were, swaying with the wind as they laughed their leafy heads off from their grand heights. Big teardrops rained from the blue sky of my eyes onto my keyboard.

Shaking and sobbing, I left my office, hurried down two flights of stairs to the main entrance of the building, and walked outside. Overwhelmed, I looked up and cried and sobbed and laughed hysterically. I finally understood what I had not been able to grasp on the top of the mountain—everything had been take care of—exactly as the oak tree had spoken. A flood of relief and gratitude rushed through my body to wash away the debris of anxiety and doubt, while I repeated, "Thank you, thank you!" over and over. Beaming, the trees stood tall and proud around me and waited for a moment longer before speaking their silent words, "We told you, but you were not listening." Then, like a fresh breeze, their whisper smiled inside my heart, and they continued, "Dear child, you are never alone," and added, "now wipe away those tears and go for it—there is a lot of work to do."

Chapter N

Appreciation and gratitude create beauty.

Gratitude transcended is joy. Pure joy heals the world.

~ Something to Re-member ~

No knowledge is ever lost; nothing can ever be forgotten. Carefully held by the trees, the memory of our knowledge is continually scribed by the land. How do we know it once more? We need to forget what we think we know to remember what we truly do know. We need to remember that memory, in its distinctiveness, is never a private something that belongs to one; rather, it is a shared heritage constantly reimagined in the body of the whole. Flickering in the space of experience between all kinds of relationships, memory is a dynamic witness to all relating. Our remembering of relationships mineralizes the bones of the future, the endless possibilities for the exchange of intrinsic vibrancies, growing afresh in becoming something of another. Hence, nothing is ever forgotten, only constantly re-membered from a matrix of information that sparks the future into present being. We are here to remember the future, reverberating whole galaxies toward us as we breathe in.

We have all come across truly inspiring people and admired them for how they contributed to our growth, deeply moving us with the words and deeds they gifted. We say that they were *born* to be prodigious artists, remarkable leaders, or simply extraordinary human beings. We speak of them as if they were *made* for what they did, as they lived their passion and fulfilled their purpose.

In much the same way, the plant *Mimosa pudica* was born to be a grand performer. The weird performance that accompanies this plant's behavior, especially her distinctive ability to play dead by suddenly folding up her leaves and drooping in reaction to touch or nightfall, has captured our attention since ancient times and ignited the flames of our imagination for centuries.[1] Over centuries of historical and cultural changes in social values and meanings, *Mimosa* has reinvented herself many times over to portray many roles and, in the process, acquired many names. Even when she was known as the "anonymous" plant, she remained in the limelight, as naturalists could not resist devoting a few pages of their journals to describe the fact that this nameless plant did not like to be touched.[2]

Decades before Carl Linnaeus established his binomial nomenclature—the modern system of naming organisms—and formally named her, the plant had risen to fame under a whole range of names, including the "living plant" *(herba viva),* the "love plant" *(herba amoris),* the "sensitive plant" *(herba sentiente),* the "sentient plant" *(planta sentiens),* the "chaste plant" *(herba casta),* the "modest plant" *(herba pudica),* the "wanton plant" *(herba delicata),* and the "bashful plant" *(herba verecunda).*[3] Also at this same time, she had already been referred to by the generic name of *Mimosa,* which derived from the Greek *mimos* and fittingly meant "mime" or "actor," but also "clown."[4] Eventually, in 1735, Carl Linnaeus formalized the scientific name of this plant as *Mimosa pudica,* while we all settled for the vernacular name of "sensitive plant." But just as a rose would smell as sweet even if called by another name,[5] so *Mimosa pudica* continued being a consummate artist, playing her part regardless of what we called her.

Indeed, after so many names and so many centuries, her qualities have remained so mesmerizing and remarkable to us that writers and scientists alike have continued making additions to her already long list of monikers: the "puzzling plant," the "action plant," and most recently, the "intelligent plant."[6] Personally, I have come to think of her as the "disobedient plant"—one who has persisted in her defiant act of not conforming to our expectations of what it means to be a *plant* and, more generally, *living.*

In fact, *Mimosa's* powerful performance of folding and unfolding her leaves in a way that reminds us of the purposeful movement of animals has succeeded at creating a strange and extraordinary bridge between two kingdoms of life—the animal and the vegetal, the sensitive and the insensitive.[7] The line that separates these two kingdoms is one we conjured a long time ago to ease our insistent need to categorize biological life forms in relative groups, as we pondered the place of the human in their midst. In 2011, *Mimosa pudica* crossed that line once again. And she was caught red-handed (or green-leafed, I should say) by scientific onlookers, much like paparazzi might catch a celebrity's most candid, even awkward, moment on film.

Fittingly, we met in Italy, *Mimosa* and I. Earlier that year, I had been awarded a research collaboration grant by my university to develop a new project with colleagues at the University of Florence, and a few months later, there I was in the famous Renaissance city. And how appropriate and true-to-form that it would be Florence, where so many prodigious scientists had laid the foundation for the modern understanding of science and, similarly, where so many brilliant actors had showcased their virtuosity in the unique improvised style of the *commedia dell'arte,*[8] which had a lasting influence on modern theater.

It was late September when the three-inch-tall plants made their first appearance on the stage of my provisional research space at the Department of Plant, Soil, and Environmental Science at the University of Florence. The experimental room I had prepared a few days prior to their arrival was like a walk-in cooler consisting of three compartments, separated from each other by curtains of black plastic. I had monitored the ambient humidity and temperature in each compartment to make sure all plants would be exposed to the same environment (patchy microenvironments could have muddled their performance). As part of my experiment, I had fitted the side compartments with fluorescent lights to produce low light (LL) conditions in one and high light (HL) conditions in the other. Finally, I had randomly assigned each plant to either the LL or HL compartment and then left them all undisturbed to settle in.

Five days later, I wrote in my lab notebook, "September 27. All plants are looking healthy and happy." I followed this with several pages of preliminary data from pilot trials, which allowed me to work out the details of the best methodology and approach to use; this would give me a feel for what may or may not work before designing the stage (Figure 3) and performing the proper full-blown experiment. I built a mechanism that would allow me to perform a "controlled drop" of the little plants, a vertical steel rail with a sliding cup. An individual plant in its pot would be put in the cup, and the cup would slide quickly down the rail fifteen centimeters, not fast enough to damage the plant, but fast enough to "scare" *Mimosa* and trigger the rapid closure of her delicate leaves—an instinctual reflex to mechanical disturbance believed to be a natural defense tactic to reduce the effects from predation. By repeatedly dropping individual plants from a set height of fifteen centimeters every five seconds, for a total of sixty drops per session—and then again and again in recurrent sessions, the stage was set.

The purpose behind building this "controlled drop system" was straightforward. To create the conditions that would make it possible, on the one hand, for the plants to perform a simple but clear task (leaf folding) that was visually detectable and quantifiable (if present) as the features typical of systems capable of true memory and learning. The question I was posing was "simple"—could *Mimosa* truly learn from new experiences and flexibly alter her behavior? Specifically, could this plant stop simply reacting (in a somewhat automatic and predetermined manner) to a disturbance that appeared to be a threat at first but quickly proved to cause no harm? These basic questions underscored a phenomenon known as

72

"habituation," which is considered the simplest form of learning, though there is nothing simple about it. Let me explain.

Instinctive behavior is an evolutionary survival mechanism developed by the members of a given species through innumerable generations of natural selection. It is the acquired habitus of the species, one that has become deeply ingrained over the evolutionary history of that species because it helped it survive. And clearly, the leaf-closing reflex of *Mimosa* is an excellent example of this. As part of her instinctive behavioral repertoire, this reflex is encoded in the DNA for the exact reason that it has proven to be extremely valuable for the survival of the species. And, like all reflexes, *Mimosa's* leaf-folding trick helps the plant respond quickly to perceived trouble and protect her from harm.

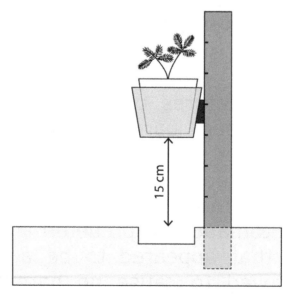

Figure 3. Controlled drop system for habituation training of Mimosa plants. The controlled drop system consisted of a plastic

vessel mounted with variable hangers onto a marked steel rail, which was, in turn, secured to a foam base. Tightly fitted in the host vessel, individual potted plants were manually elevated to the fifteen-centimeter height mark and allowed to drop by sliding along the rail. The shallow depression in the foam base at the landing point of the vessel prevented it from bouncing at impact. The set-up ensured that a standard level of disturbance was administered to all plants, and it was sufficient to force the closure of all leaves. Figure reproduced from: M. Gagliano, M. Renton, M. Depczynski, and S. Mancuso, "Experience Teaches Plants to Learn Faster and Forget Slower in Environments Where It Matters," Oecologia 175 (2014): 63–72.

But herein lies the twist in the story—*Mimosa's* defensive behavior does not come for free. The leaf-folding reflex is "survival-friendly" only when the threat is real. When *Mimosa* folds her leaves shut, her capacity to forage for light suddenly plunges by half, and the "survival-unfriendly" risk of starvation becomes a reality. This makes the reflex an exorbitant living expense—a justifiable one to pay if the danger is real, but a downright waste of precious opportunities to forage for light and thrive when a situation turns out to be not dangerous at all. Because of this trade-off between predation risk and energy gain, it seems unreasonable to think that *Mimosa* would have little or no control over her own behavior; that the plant would be incapable of assessing what circumstances demand and offer; and that she would be unable to learn from experience, unable to learn to ignore the harmless nuisance of, for example, a controlled drop, to spare herself the unnecessary trouble (and energy loss) of closing her leaves. And yet at the time of the experiment, the general assumption was that plants could respond *only* in preprogrammed and automatic ways already encoded into their DNA, that they were somehow being acted *upon* rather than acting in their own right. *Mimosa* had her mind set on changing this view, and I was simply her stage manager, light engineer, and voice to allow her performance to roll out. At the time, however, I had not realized that she had planned to do this by way of a clever five-act Shakespearean production!

After a few days of trial and error, I had a pretty good idea of what needed doing, and with all props rigged up and rehearsal time over, everything was ready for the grand opening performance. And as in any theater worthy of its name, the young plants were held out of view behind a dark curtain in the side compartments of my Italian laboratory, waiting in trepidation for their time to appear on the main stage (the middle compartment), where their performance would be put to the test—to close, or not to close, that was the question! Would *Mimosa* perceive the occurrence of the inconsequential drop and tune it out to focus on the things that really demanded attention? Would she remember what she had learned (if that was at all possible), and if so, for how long? *Mimosa* answered it all with a moving display of wide-open leaves through five separate acts.

Act 1: The Instinctual Response. A group of sixteen naïve plants (eight from the LL compartment and eight from the HL one) makes an initial appearance on the main stage first thing in the morning of October 3, 2011. One by one, each plant is gently placed in the plastic vessel mounted onto the marked steel rail of the controlled drop system and dropped. Each plant is dropped only once in the morning; a brief, single drop is then administered again eight hours later on the same day. Did *Mimosa* learn from a single drop? No. All plants completely folded their leaves in the morning and did exactly the same later in the day. And rightly so—a better-safe-than-sorry approach was undoubtedly the most appropriate response to the new, undefined, and potentially dangerous circumstances. Besides, such a fleeting and limited experience offered no opportunities for evaluating whether the nuisance was or wasn't a threat to survival. So nothing to learn, nothing to remember.

Act 2: The Learned Response. A new group of fifty-six naïve plants (twenty-eight from the LL compartment and twenty-eight from the HL one) enters the main stage one by one, and each is individually dropped using the controlled drop system. This time, however, each plant is not dropped only once at the start and once at the end of the day; instead, each plant is dropped sixty times at five-second intervals and experiences six of these sixty-drop training sessions spread throughout the whole day. Did *Mimosa* learn now? Yes (maybe). As before, all plants instinctively folded their leaves at the first few drops, quickly responding to the potential of danger while waiting for the true nature of their circumstances to become more defined. However, remarkably, the initial four to six drops was all they needed to suss out the situation and come to the conclusion that being dropped was an annoyance, perhaps, but certainly not a threat and thus could be safely ignored. As that happened, all plants started reopening their leaves even while I continued dropping them to the end of their sixty-drop training session. Not only were their leaves completely open by the end of that first session, but they also stopped closing altogether even on the first drop at successive training sessions as the day progressed. Perhaps even more unsurprisingly, given the trade-off between predation risk and energetic gain described above, plants kept under the more demanding conditions of the low light (LL) compartment actually learned more rapidly and reopened more fully than those from the high light (HL) compartment. How exciting to have the habituation experiment setting off to such a great start as *Mimosa* quickly learned to stop reacting to being dropped!

As in any good story, however, it was at this point that the first hurdle appeared. Sure, *Mimosa* stopped closing her leaves, but had the plant truly learned to ignore the drop because of the repeated exposure and was now "choosing" to keep her leaves open? Or was she just pooped out and physically no longer capable of closing them? There was a way to find out, and it required *Mimosa* to pass an additional test, one where a brand-new stimulus could elicit the leaf closure if the plants were not fatigued but still responsive to what was going on in their surrounding environment. This was aptly known as the *dis*habituation test.

Act 3: The Dishabituation Challenge. There they were, on the main stage: the fifty-six plants that had somehow decided to stop closing their leaves. After six consecutive training sessions of sixty drops each, the young plants were now going to face a new challenge. One at a time, each *Mimosa* was placed in a close-fitting foam container attached to a vibrating plate, one of those commonly found in chemistry labs and used to mix liquids. Each plant was placed on the plate and gently vibrated for a brief five seconds. The vibrating plate was a good choice of stimulus for the dishabituation test because, as scientific protocol demands, it did not differ significantly in kind from the vertical drop—both disturbances being mechanical in nature—but it was, nonetheless, absolutely new to the plant.

By virtue of its novelty, the vibrations were expected to elicit the rapid leaf-folding reflex as effectively as the drop had done at the very beginning, unless, of course, *Mimosa* had actually lost the capacity to move due to exhaustion and thus was physically unable to close in response to, well, anything. This is an important distinction. From an ecological perspective, the inability to respond appropriately to unfamiliar and sporadic stimuli would be extremely dangerous. It would leave the plant unguarded in the face of potentially harmful circumstances, but this undesirable situation is not what happened here to our actors. When vibrated, without exception, all leaves folded up completely, indicating that *Mimosa* was not fatigued at all. Instead, she was totally capable of detecting and responding to a new stimulus and remained responsive to what was new and potentially threatening.

While a fantastic outcome, *Mimosa's* response to the brief, one-off experience of the vibrations was not enough (at least for science). If *Mimosa* had truly habituated to the original vertical drop and had learned of its benign nature from previous experience, she should have the capacity to ignore it when re-confronted by it. So once more, down went the young plants, sliding along the steel rail of the controlled drop system to land softly in the shallow foam depression at its base. As in a gesture of triumph, they all stood proud and tall and kept their leaves wide open the entire distance, passing their new test with flying colors. Then one-by-one they returned to their respective backstage areas, behind the curtains, to rest from their day's performance.

Act 4: The Remembering. After so much falling down and standing tall, the question of *Mimosa's* learning seemed settled. Well, almost. The interesting thing about science and scientists is that they are simultaneously curious and natural skeptics, the latter a pattern reinforced by the scientific process at every step of the way. So my question was, how far can I push this? How capable are these wondrous little plants, really? For us, learning from a past experience is contingent on the ability to recall that memory, and unless the information is encoded and stored where it is available to be used again, it would be really hard to function in everyday life. Think of touching a hotplate. For this reason, memory is integral for successful learning to take place.

So the question of *Mimosa's* learning was, in actuality, a question of whether the plants could remember what they had previously experienced—in the absence of a brain in which to retain memory. After passing their dishabituation test, all fifty-six plants had returned to their respective backstage compartments behind the curtains for three undisturbed days off. Then, half of them (fourteen from the LL compartment and fourteen from the HL one) would make their reappearance onto the main stage to be presented once more with the vertical drop. Incredibly, when they did, nothing happened. That was the most perfect and exciting "nothing" that I could have hoped for. The behavioral response they had acquired three days earlier was unchanged: leaves open before the drop, leaves open after the drop. Like seasoned little base jumpers, these plants continued to disregard the drop as they had learned to do during their training, and by ignoring it now, they were showing me they could remember the drop flawlessly. They had the faculty of memory, and their behavior was not hard-wired in DNA, but learned! How amazing!

I was left awed and numb with the significance of my results. Three days later, I tried again. I tested the second half of the original group, plants that, by then, had been left undisturbed behind the curtains for a total of six days. The twenty-eight plants returned to the main stage and were presented again with the vertical drop. Here something quite interesting occurred. All plants remembered the drop, but their specific environments influenced how well they did so. As mentioned before, plants that close their leaves in the absence of a real threat are wasting precious opportunities to forage for light and flourish. However, making such a mistake carries a heavier price tag for survival when vital resources such as light are in short supply, which was the case for the fourteen plants that had been kept under low light conditions. These plants retained the behavioral response acquired earlier practically unchanged, disregarding the drop a full six days after their last experience of it. Out of necessity, they were the faster learners and retained the learned behavior longer when compared to their companions held under the more favorable conditions in the HL compartment. These, too, disregarded the drop stimulus but were not as quick at reopening their leaves or as good at reopening them as fully, precisely because the energetic consequences of little blunders were not such a big deal in an environment with abundant light at their disposal.

I decided to test all the plants once again, but with another twist—a student-exchange program of sorts. I swapped the respective environments so that half of the plants that had been trained while being held in the LL compartment were now transferred to the HL one, and vice versa. After twenty-eight days in their new environment, they returned to the main stage to be retested. One more time, they kept their leaves open while ignoring the nuisance of being dropped, gratuitously. The lesson had definitely been learned and remembered. And so?

Act 5: The Great Re-membering. As the opening of *Mimosa's* performance had been accompanied by understandable trepidation and an initial stage fright (which, no doubt, was part of the performance itself!), so the closing act was delivered with a sense of triumphant accomplishment (hers) and surprise (mine). Unfolding like any mythical hero's journey,[9] both accomplishment and surprise would take several years to fully reveal themselves as newly unearthed old bones. The curtains of this final act had to wait for a while before coming down completely—waiting for us to hear our own story being told. Then, leaving us with a new sense of who we really are, the emerging wisdom could return us home, to the place where we had started the journey, but which we now truly knew for the first time.[10]

The results of the "*Mimosa* experiment," as it has come to be known around the world, were an amazing and altogether incredibly exciting scientific breakthrough. But my lack of success in communicating these exciting results was a frustrating journey that took a lot of the shine off it for me. I started doubting whether my results and their significance could be communicated at all. It seemed as if what *Mimosa* was presenting to us was altogether too far removed from our established reality not just as scientists but, indeed, as humans. How can a plant learn, learn so fast, remember, and act according to its individual circumstances? Was it too unbelievable for others to even conceive of? Was it only me who was completely astounded by the performance of *Mimosa?*

In January 2014, following years of scathing remarks by many peers, the research paper describing the experiment was finally published.[11] The date marked the end of a long series of rejections by over a dozen major academic journals, which would not even send the manuscript out for peer review and would quickly brush it off (in some cases, without even reading it) with one of those off-the-shelf impersonal responses, such as "we receive many more manuscripts that we can publish" or "the topic is outside the scope of the journal."

Of course, skepticism, resistance, and even blatant hostility to the idea that plants could truly learn and remember were not completely unanticipated.[12] Although knowing this never succeeded at tempering the sharp edges of rejection, it did help me see something I had not, in fact, expected. It seemed that, no matter which side of the fence one sat on, the notion of plant learning, memory, and decision making (and the matters of subjectivity and agency that the occurrence of these processes was ushering in) had caught everyone off guard. We were somewhat unrehearsed for the play *Mimosa* had put on and which—candidly unprepared or stubbornly unwilling—we all were, nevertheless, characters of.

As scientists, we are habituated, for the most part, to speak of the structure of things in terms of immediate mechanical, physical, physiological, and biochemical/molecular factors (i.e., investigating the "how does it work?" question).[13] It is unsurprising, then, that the questions and arguments that were most readily offered in response to the *Mimosa* experiment reflected this well-entrenched perspective. Processes such as learning and memory are explained and understood by the physiological mechanisms that underwrite them. For example, long-term memory can be described in relation to changes in synaptic connectivity expressed in the brain and, to a certain extent, speak of the synapse as a cellular site for memory storage, a site that interacts with a wide range of molecules across complex networks. Understood from this perspective, memory is inevitably contingent on the existence of a brain. And from here, we've painted ourselves into a corner—we have no choice but to stumble forward by formulating increasingly frail arguments to advance our knowledge, such as, "Plants have no brain and no synapses to retain memory; therefore, how can they do any actual remembering?" How limiting. Besides, this intriguing question harbors the insinuating (ill)logic that a plant cannot. Not being open to consider the very nature of our reasoning and assumptions regarding the relationship between brains and memories leaves us no space to seek other possibilities. As though embodying an instinct toward self-preservation, the question leaves no space to be questioned, no space for us to see that, essentially, it is the formulation of the question itself that has been failing us all along.

Possibly because my research interests and training had always been ecologically and environmentally focused, the questions I wanted to ask were naturally broader, more inclusive, and process-oriented—asking "*why* does it occur?" rather than "*how* does it occur?" (I admit that I have more limited skills for the latter question. I leave mechanisms to the physiologists!) In the context of this background, I didn't see memory, for example, as a fixed trait of the organism, something that belonged to that organism and could be explained and reduced to specific chemical compounds. Because memories are born of and come into existence within and through relationships of all kinds, as an ecologist, I saw memory as a feature of a truly ecological, dynamic process of relationships, where meanings emerge to shape the production of behaviors that, in turn, shape new interactions for new meanings to emerge. Thus, I was excited about the role memory played in shaping the plant's behavior—how *Mimosa* approached different circumstances by both remembering the past and encountering the present and then expressed the relative meaning through informed action.

Conversely, I felt quite uninterested in the *how* questions that seemed to insist in shriveling such an active and ecologically vibrant process to the finite dimension for cells on Petri dishes and molecules in Eppendorf tubes. It is through this reductionist approach that the subjective plant, made of raw, vibrant living flesh,[14] had been dismembered, disincarnated, and substituted with a lackluster abstraction, the scientific idea of what an objectified plant is, does, and knows. An idea is not the plant, in the same way that the idea I may have of you is not actually you, but a simplified, broken-down version of you. And to me, this is far from a trivial point. The disarticulation of plants as subjects and their cultural (re)construction as objects of scientific exploration not only contradicts the emerging and expanded understanding of plant behavior, including matters of plant intelligence, agency, and intersubjectivity, but is also of monumental concern in regards to the ethical significance of human-plant relations.[15]

Against this backdrop, *Mimosa* had accomplished the extraordinary. By re-membering her disarticulated vegetal body,[16] she had prodded directly at an internal contradiction, one of a most profound state of deso*u*lation that demands we de-vegetalize the plant and dehumanize the human in order to stomach its Orwellian poison.[17] By pointing at the agonizing convulsions in the belly of the plant-human relationship, *Mimosa* had come to initiate the process of detoxification. Perhaps, *this* was the reason why *Mimosa,* the plant—being capable of learning and remembering—made us, the human, so uncomfortable. And I was about to discover the surprising place where this discomfort enjoyed hiding inside me.

You see, along the path with *Mimosa,* I had encountered excitement and frustration, as well as the minor demigods of lesser emotions. However, the real showdown was yet to come, and it would all take place, well, by surprise. It was precisely in my own surprise that I was to find the betraying sign of the internal incoherence that makes our relationship with plants so terribly jerky. Clearly, the *Mimosa* experiment had been surprising in many ways, particularly in that it would ultimately reveal more about the human than the plant. For me, the initial surprise had materialized out of a sense of disbelief—with no brain or nervous system, *Mimosa* was breaking with convention! In my disbelief, I was excited. Farcically, however, the presence of disbelief in my response to her performance was telling a great deal (certainly greater than I first cared to recognize) about my own keeping with convention. My disbelief and surprise revealed an embedded conditioning—I expected *Mimosa* to fail. Yes, fail! And not so much because plants have no brain—a rather superficial discrimination I had drawn my own attention to at first—but simply because *they* are not *us.*

Obviously, plants and humans differ in many ways, both in structure and in function. However, how we cognize such differences is a crucial part of the equation, because, as we know well, how we think of and value differences can lead us to divergent conclusions about the way we perceive, interact with, and know the world. We seem to have a longstanding tradition of differentiating ourselves from nonhuman others through the things that those others lack.[18] Unfortunately, when we do so, we inevitably use the qualities and conditions of the nonhuman as oppositional foils—we get a plant like *Mimosa* to play the antagonist, the deficient character that struggles against us, the self-appointed hero, and, as a result, our leading role shine brighter. When we do so, at best, we fail to arrive at any convincing or meaningful conclusion about our distinctiveness, and at worst, we generate distorted beliefs about our own nature as well as that of the others—beliefs that prove disastrous for our relationship both with our own natures and with those of others.

Unaware, I was sick with this great madness—our deep-rooted anthropocentric habit of using the human as *the* reference point, the gold standard from which to measure "down" and pass judgment on the nature of those others.[19] It was my feeling of surprise that flagged those unsuspected inscriptions lurching under the safety blanket of my unconscious. When I decided to peek under that blanket and venture deeper into the disbelief I had felt, I was faced with my own implicit cultural attitudes and stereotypes.[20] Those markings were written all over the wall of my thinking and knowing about these vegetal others, and their directives confined my understanding of them to the domain of human values and perceptions.

I felt so naïve and, at the same time, so hideously parochial about the fact that my beliefs and perceptions of the world were tinted by the stinky old anthropocentric bias, despite the amazing experiences I'd had that had taught me otherwise. How little do we truly know of our nature and the nature of those around us, human and nonhuman. We keep writing books about books that debate ideas of ideas about the fundamental processes of life, such as learning and remembering, which are found everywhere and all around us—processes that are self-perpetuating and self-controlling with or without our ideas of them, stories about them, and debates over them. The case of *Mimosa's* learning is simply a no-brainer. Appreciating what *Mimosa* had accomplished requires no cerebral assumption to be applied, but rather the surrender of prejudices and biases that filter everything new we learn through the views we already hold.

It is in this surrender that I was able to realize what was truly surprising about *Mimosa.* Like a quick-witted jester at the imperial court of humanity, she had come to make fools of all of us with her leafy dexterity, clowning around our taxonomic prejudices and dogmatic judgments. She had taken our fixation—the importance we give to movement—and imitated animal reactions using her own body movements. She had clumsily "played the animal" for us, not because she is inferior and can't do "better," but to show us, by way of ridiculing, what little we see—as if the human animal cannot see that she is, indeed, *herba viva* (the living plant) unless she plays animal for us. Free from human conventions, she had pointed straight at the naked butt of the emperor to bring our vain arrogance into the open so we may see it. She expertly showed us that the definitions we apply to our world determine what we allow ourselves to see and that *un*knowingly, by way of our definitions, we end up rejecting what *is* in favor of what we have already decided it *should be.* And all the while, elusive in her plantness, she had also come with a silent invitation to our dis-education, challenged us to unlearn the distinctions we invented and cling to as if they are the only thing that define us.

It should be clear that unlearning distinctions doesn't mean not seeing them; it doesn't mean that differences are not useful. What it does mean is that we stop being obsessed with them to the point that we cannot see anything beyond them and thus miss the incredible richness of qualities and characters of both the human and the nonhuman world. It is through this unlearning that we can take those first steps away from objectifying plants and realize that recognizing their subjectivity and inherent worth and dignity does not diminish our own but rather enriches it.

When I finally understood all this, the quality of my surprise was magically transformed from a sense of disbelief born of anthropocentric conceit into a feeling of awe. It was a sense of elated wonder inspired by something sublime, something magnificent that engenders a deep reverence for life. It is awe that inspires the freedom for very different questions to be asked, questions that don't need to be answered in order to renew our sense of ecological intimacy and kinship with the nonhuman living world, to remind us that we care. And *this* is what was so truly surprising and inspiring about *Mimosa.*

Now, at this point one may expect the performance to finally find closure. The truth of the matter is, however, that the curtains of this final act may never come down completely, as *Mimosa* keeps at the task she had set herself to accomplish—to question our minds. She has certainly continued questioning and opening my mind. And—little did I know at the time—this dis-education of mine was only the start.

Chapter G

The teachings are not individual, but universal.

~ A...mazing Pea ~

Gazing in and out of a maze of illuminated landscapes, we travel across the boundless territories of an electrified mind seeking the world. Invisible to the eyes at first, the world emerges out of the formless to make an impression on the canvas of our consciousness with the swirling colors of its dancing photons. Shining outward, brushstrokes of fragmented forms are stitched together into a seamless reality, born out of the mind and seen through the eyes of our imagining. What if we were able to stretch that imagining far beyond our eyes, letting our vision travel far wider than the brushstrokes the mind has learned to comprehend...? But how can we learn the art of seeing that which we cannot yet imagine? Vision is an art, and nature an old master painter teaching us how to see the underlying reality of things to be—before they actually are. Unleash the mind into seeing across invisible territories; then an amazing vision will bring the as-yet-unmanifest world into being.

Landing at Pucallpa's airport felt different from the last time I had come here a few years earlier. The plants had been adamant that I come back to Peru, even if I had no real desire to do so. But there I was again. Later, somewhere in the middle of seemingly nowhere, I was spending my first afternoon back in the Amazon on the banks of the Ucayali River, listening to my new teacher, Don J, as he shared his knowledge on how he used plants to treat illnesses, pointing to a bristly plant down here and a tall and skinny one over there. A strong old man with kind eyes and not many teeth left to his smile, Don J was a Cocama shaman.[1] He had agreed to meet me in Pucallpa for a sort of job interview after a common acquaintance had put us in contact a couple of days earlier. The first thing Don J told me as we sat down for this meeting at a small café was that he had neither interest in nor the intention of teaching Westerners. Then he proceeded to ask me about my reasons for being there. "I am here because the plants have brought me here," I answered. Then, before I knew it, I added, "I need to become a better dreamer." He left without a word, but the next day he came to pick me up and take me to his home in the jungle, where I was going to diet with the plants.

That afternoon, Don J prepared a concoction made from Piñon blanco *(Jatropha curcas),* a drought-resistant shrub[2] also known as "purging nut" because of his cleansing effects on the bowels. By the time darkness descended in the jungle, I had drunk his medicine and entered the dreamscape where the spirit of this *maestro* was already awaiting to meet me. Wearing a doctor's white coat, Piñon blanco appeared in my dream as a tall, middle-aged man with short black hair and dark eyes.[3] He spoke of many things throughout the night, all the way into the first light of the morning. I paid great attention to his words, but at the same time, I knew that our discussion was somehow bypassing my mind. On the one hand, I knew exactly what he was talking to me about; on the other, my poor brain hadn't really been able to hear the words or understand them.

By the time morning came, I couldn't remember a thing Piñon blanco had said. I spoke with Don J about it. Images and details started flooding my awareness, and abruptly I found myself saying, "He was holding a fruit-like thing in his hand"—my hands were wildly gesturing the "something" I had seen as if I were playing a game of charades. Giving away his childlike delight, Don J's almost toothless smile signaled that he was pleased to hear my description of that which, to me, remained a mysterious "something." "I know what it is!" he said with great satisfaction. "It is a very powerful medicine. You will need to bathe with it and drink it, but only a little." And then he added, "you will diet it once you finish the work with this *doctorcito.*"

As Don J had mentioned the day before, while looking at the plants growing around his hut, the plant spirits themselves teach us what to do, including what plants one is ready to diet. By showing me this strange fruit that looked like a cannonball, Piñon blanco had told me about the plant that was waiting to work with me next. And ready she was, the mighty Ayahuma.[4]

"The experiment is pretty simple. Train young plants in a maze and give them the freedom of choice," Ayahuma declared, inside my head. Then she added, "But you've got to think peas, not sunflowers!" For several months earlier that year, I had tried to design an experiment that would allow me to test plants' ability for associative learning—also known as Pavlovian learning, after the famous experiments of Pavlov and his dogs.[5] The idea was to test whether plants were capable of learning that the occurrence of one event was not only somehow linked to another but also, more importantly, anticipated it. How to actually test this in plants was something that I had stubbornly been thinking about since 2011, as a follow-up to the study with *Mimosa pudica.*

For this purpose, the shed behind my home in Perth had been turned into a carpenter's workshop (and a free-of-charge sauna, courtesy of the scorching Western Australian summer!). Together with Martial—my best friend and long-term collaborator—I had designed and built some "learning boxes," which we had then brought into my lab at the university for testing. Each box was made of plywood, equipped with a timer controlling the activity of a fan, included a light source, and was fitted with a camera taking time-lapse photographs of sunflower seedlings supposedly making their "choices." I was convinced that we had created the perfect system for a Pavlovian learning test in plants, but it simply didn't work! Despite much frustration and time spent mulling over it, I just couldn't figure out why my apparently perfect setup wasn't working! Well, until *she* pointed it out....

Ayahuma *(Couroupita guianensis)* is a tree native to the tropical forests of northeastern South America, where is it held in high regard by the shamans of the Amazon Basin region. How this tall, spectacular beauty made it out of the South American jungle and into the Indian subcontinent and Southeast Asia is still a mystery,[6] but there too, this extraordinary tree holds a special significance in the mythologies of the place and is often found growing at religious sites. In India, for example, the tree is commonly planted as a guardian at the entrance of Shiva temples;[7] in countries like Sri Lanka and Thailand, its evergreen presence stands glorious outside Buddhist temples as a symbol of enlightenment.[8]

Away from its Amazonian home, Ayahuma is better known by its English moniker, cannonball tree—and aptly so. Not only are the fruits large, spherical, and as heavy as their namesakes, but also, as they ripen, they come plummeting to the ground with loud and explosive noises. One may be glad to know that signs are often posted near cannonball trees that have been planted in urban settings warning people to keep at a safe distance to avoid serious head injuries. Ironically, the spirit of Ayahuma was set on that very task—not exactly to crack my head open, but my mind, no doubt. Of course, I had no idea of that at the time, but she did nonetheless. Pragmatic and down-to-earth, Ayahuma intended to unleash a vision that was lying dormant and out of sight in the labyrinth of my mind. Just like her fruits, which do not release their seeds until they fall down to the earth, I was ripening to fall thunderously to the ground of academic science and to burst open and fire my seeds of wild ideas into material existence. But just as her fruits do not continue to ripen if picked prematurely, it was essential that I wait for the right time.

Don J cracked a cannonball fruit open to expose the inner pulp. Inside, the gelatinous and alien-like flesh was peppered by a multitude of black seeds; left exposed to oxygen, the pulp turns bluish-purple. Apparently, these fruits are just about inedible—the pulp is known to cause allergies, and its notorious putrid smell is quite a deterrent for humans.[9] Don

J mixed it in water for me to bathe in, so as to begin my *dieta* with her. And later that night I did, standing naked under the loyal watch of a cacao tree, whose reassuring presence gave me the deep inner poise I surely needed in that jungle-raw moment. First I faced the easterly direction of the rising sun as Don J poured the lovely "soup" over my head and shrouded me in the white smoke of his *mapacho,* while I proceeded rubbing my whole body with the foul mixture. Then I faced the westerly direction of the setting sun, and more of the stinky concoction washed over me, and more tobacco smoke enveloped my bare body, which was now shivering in the nocturnal coolness of the jungle. I dried myself off, put some clothes back on, and drank a small glass filled to the rim with the Ayahuma's water. Then I walked back to my bed and went to sleep with fruity tidbits still entangled in my hair, where they remained for the following week, during which time I was not allowed to wash.

Left in complete isolation inside the confines of the mosquito net that hung over my thin mattress, I spent that first day of my *dieta* dry fasting and drifting in and out of sleep. Not put off by the pungent stench of Ayahuma in my hair, the spirits of the plants I had dieted over the years returned within my dreams. Their arrival was accompanied by a warm sense of reassurance—I was glad to retrieve the medicine of my past *dietas* and know that the relationships I had secured with those plant spirits were still there, after all.

That is when she arrived. "There is nothing for you to acquire, only to remember," said Ayahuma. "Watch those false ideas planted inside your mind. Each false idea is a delusion created by a solidified thought pattern, an insane habit that keeps your attention fixed. But nothing is fixed; everything is fluctuating, changing, evolving...." Before I could ask how you get rid of these false ideas, she answered with one simple but enigmatic instruction: "Turn in to find the curse of a false idea within the idea itself." And with that, she disappeared, and I woke up. It has taken me years to start grasping what Ayahuma shared and to begin to recognize the insanity of my delusion. The madness she pointed out truly is the work of a master trickster, a Machiavellian sleight-of-hand pulling the wool over the eyes of the innocent mind. Like a noxious weed planted in the most pristine imaginative ground, the delusion takes hold to fix the mind in place, immobilized into a place of anxious preoccupation. Then, through a socially perpetuated conditioning system, the pure knowing of our infinite nature is squandered in exchange for the penitentiary of a *distorted* awareness. Not long ago, this vertiginous insanity all of a sudden became clear, thanks to my encounter with an extraordinary shaman.[10] To my amusement, I have just found out that in folk medicine, Ayahuma is said to bring someone mad back to sanity. Unquestionably, she had intended to set me on the right track.

Ayahuma is widely recognized as a mighty protector and teacher. Although this tree is typically considered a powerful *maestro*—the gender of the noun implying masculinity—the spirit often also appears as a giant woman and, specifically, one without a head. I never actually glimpsed at her ethereal form (headless or not)—but this wonderfully quirky and buoyant spirit enjoyed playing with my head (in the most benevolent of ways!) and educating my mind. To do so, she made sure I could hear her voice loud and clear when she started prescribing the complete set of instructions for testing Pavlovian learning in plants. I transcribed as she dictated. And literally, this is how the pages of my travel diary filled up with the words she spoke and the diagrams she sketched. Upon my return home to Australia, those words and sketches started growing, extending their plant-like runners beyond the pages where they had been seeded and out into my lab. There, eventually, they flowered into the pioneering experiments that they had been conceived to be all along.

At the Plant Growth Facilities at the University of Western Australia, I transformed one of the controlled-environment rooms into my plant-learning laboratory. The room was meticulously kept in complete darkness at all times; all light switches were taped over to prevent anyone from accidentally turning the lights on. A thick sheet of black plastic—the kind builders use under concrete—was secured over the entrance to prevent light from coming in when someone opened the door. A sign on the door warned, "Plant learning in progress. Do not enter." This, of course, made some researchers working within the same facility curious about what was going on. Some ventured to ask, but it was never clear to me whether they really heard my answer. "I am trying to teach pea seedlings some tricks," I would say mischievously. I would then wait for puzzlement to creep across their faces before adding, "Yeah, you know, just as you would train your puppy with tasty treats."

The irony was that I was far from joking. In fact, it was by studying his dogs that Ivan Pavlov—in one of the most revealing studies in the history of behavioral research—had demonstrated that behavior could be changed using conditioning. In these experiments, Pavlov's dogs had learned to associate the ringing of a bell with the imminent arrival of dinner to the point where the sound of the bell alone made the dogs salivate in anticipation of dinner. Would my little peas learn that the position of a small fan—the equivalent to the ringing bell—rightly predicted the time and place for the occurrence of the only light made available to them—their dinner?

As instructed by Ayahuma, I set up a simple series of experiments by placing pea seedlings in individual Y-shaped mazes constructed out of PVC pipes (Figure 4). During training, as each seedling grew inside its maze, I exposed them first to the gentle breeze of a small fan (as a neutral conditioning cue) followed by light (food), a biologically significant cue, which was offered as a kind of reward. For three consecutive days, I repeated this on different arms of the maze, though fan and light always appeared on the same side of the maze in one experimental group and on opposite sides in another group. On the fourth day, I tested their ability to learn by association by turning on the fan alone. Just as in Pavlov's experiment, in which the bell acquired meaning when the dogs learned that it predicted dinner, the fan in my experiment had no meaning to the peas to start with. So the question was whether it would acquire meaning if the peas learned of its significance. It did, though I almost didn't see it.

Two weeks passed. I was in my lab, monitoring peas and setting up mazes, lights, and fans, every single day from the early hours of the morning till late in the afternoon. Technically, the experimental system was working well, and the peas were successfully growing, but their ability to navigate the maze didn't seem to be influenced by the presence of the fan as the cue that would give them the best chance at finding light. The initial data suggested that about half of the seedlings were growing to the left and half to the right of the maze in a random fashion (50:50). In short, they were failing the test.

102

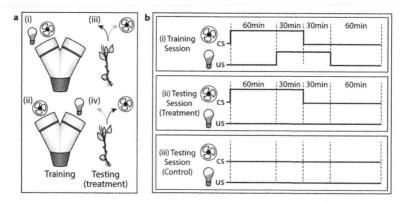

Figure 4. Training and testing protocol for associative learning in pea seedlings. (a) During training seedlings were exposed to the fan [F] and light [L] on either the same arm (i) or on the opposite arm (ii) of the Y-maze. The fan served as the conditioned stimulus (CS), light as the unconditioned stimulus (US). During testing with exposure to the fan alone, two categories of responses were distinguished. Correct response: Seedlings growing into the arm of the maze where the light was "predicted" by the fan to occur [green arrow; iii (corresponding to scenario i) and iv (corresponding to scenario ii)]; Incorrect response: Seedlings growing into the arm of the maze where the light was not "predicted" by the fan to occur (black arrow; iii and iv). (b) Seedlings received training for three consecutive days before testing. Each training day consisted of three two-hour training sessions separated by one-hour intervals. The ninety-minute CS preceded the sixty-minute US by sixty minutes so that there was a thirty-minute overlap. (i). During the one-day testing session, seedlings were exposed to the fan alone for three ninety-minute sessions (ii). Seedlings of the control group were left undisturbed (no fan, no light; iii). Figure originally published in: M. Gagliano, V.V. Vyazovskiy, A.A. Borbély, M. Grimonprez, and M. Depczynski, "Learning by Association in Plants," Scientific Reports 6 (2016): article number 38427.

Head low and tail between my legs, there I was on a sunny Sunday morning ready to dismantle and pack away the whole setup, dismayed at the outcome. I left the brightness of the outside world and walked into the dim light of the Plant Growth Facilities' corridor. I opened the door marked "Plant learning in progress. Do not enter." and entered. The controlled-environment room met me with its computerized wave of coolness, which rolled over my skin until I broke into a shiver. The room absorbed me within its undisturbed darkness, where several pea seedlings were quietly waiting inside their mazes. At the flick of one switch, the tiny blue LED lights mounted on each maze glowed like fireflies in the rich blackness of the space, a space where the confinement of walls had become imperceptible.

I glanced around as my inquisitorial mind started the court-martial. How could I have been so daft? Did I seriously believe that a tree in the Amazon—or, to be precise, the *spirit* of a tree in the Amazon—had given me instructions (which, to my credit, I had followed to a T) on how to carry out these experiments? All of a sudden, as the internal assault escalated, my eyes stopped searching. My gaze brushed over a little something that, until that moment, had gone unnoticed. There in the dark, I had found what I had been looking for.

We believe we see only because of the presence of light, but it is in the dark that light becomes visible. From the encounter of light and darkness we are born, and with us, the world emerges. Constantly molding the world around us with our gaze, we in turn are molded by the gaze the world presses upon us. Unaware of this interplay of luminosities, we rarely recognize that all we see is seeing us. Rarely do we realize that by virtue of its being all around us, the penetrating gaze of the world sees us, at all times and from all sides, in our multidimensionality. We, however, see the world from a one-sided standpoint only: the frontal view. As in single-point perspective drawing, we make the object of our most immediate gaze look realistic and three-dimensional, while most of the world is distorted and lost away to a vanishing point in an illusory distance.

Except on specific occasions, the vegetality of the world seems to be relegated precisely to that distant and imaginary background of our perception. It's perception that—to use the elegant words of philosopher Michael Marder—is the "key passageway for the body's openness to the world and the world's reception by the body."[11] In this openness, as time disappears, our relationship with space is all that matters. No longer separate from the exteriority of our milieu, the world around us ceases to be the *world* in the agreed sense of the word. Effervescing with evanescent and yet endless extemporizations, the world births itself visible in a remarkable fluidity of both composing and decomposing, becoming and undoing. It is in this liminal space of pure possibility, where the being-made meets the coming-undone, where light encounters darkness, that we, too, are conceived. It is here that we wait, not knowing, to encounter the other, to become the other, and—exactly as the *planta maestra* Socoba had susurrated—it is here that we, humans, become them, plants. Can conventional science ever render this *un*knowing knowable, this *in*visible visible? And can we ever unravel our encounters without disrupting the integrity of the other whom we meet? Or is "disruption" a space for mutual transformation, hence a vital element in the encounter? On that Sunday morning, the peas seedlings were waiting in my lab, not to tell me *if,* but show me *how.*

My gaze dawdled over one of the mazes. Time stopped. I found myself simply being—being there with the vegetal presence inside the maze, attending to this presence in the darkness. Suspended in the empty space between expectations, a new configuration of ideas and relations emerged. And in that darkness, I saw it clearly. I was "within the vegetal experience" and able to discern and define that which enabled the green tendril of my young peas to stretch toward the dark in order to find the light. "Holy shit, they are doing it after all!" I squealed. I looked over, inside the maze, once again. I squealed again. My heart was beating furiously, and I started feeling lightheaded. I checked another maze, then another, as an overwhelming exhilaration burst up and outward into luminous tears. The young plants were correctly predicting the imminent arrival of light *(when)* and its direction *(where)* based on the presence and position of the neutral conditioning stimulus, the fan; in response, they were directing their slender vegetal forms into that arm of the maze. In astonishment, I speed-walked right out of the blackness of the controlled-environment room, into the dim light of the Plant Growth Facilities' corridor, and out into the bright sunlight of that Sunday morning, still repeating aloud, "They're doing it! They're doing it!"

The disquieting irony of the whole situation was that the plants had performed their associative task correctly from the word go, and I had not recognized it. How was it possible I had missed this? I had looked after the young peas in their mazes every single day for a whole two weeks. How could it be that until that moment I had been incapable of seeing how wonderfully they were learning?

The reason for this was pretty straightforward, at least on the surface. The peas were not incompetent at learning; they were simply failing to satisfy the regime of expectations that I (and many other behavioral scientists) had been trained to look out for, that being that a comparison be made using random choice—a hypothetical expectation that, without learning, half of the seedlings would simply grow to the left and half to the right of the maze. According to this expectation, it would be said that the plants had learned to use the fan (conditioned stimulus) as a reliable indicator of future light if a (statistical) majority much greater than 50 percent grew toward the fan. Because the number of seedlings that did grow toward the fan was only slightly more than what one may expect by random chance, I had concluded that they were not able to learn by association. What I had missed, however, was that this hypothetical expectation was incorrect to start with, simply because this is not what *real* pea seedlings that have been exposed to light actually do! It was not their baseline behavior. Their natural behavior is to consistently grow in the direction where light was last experienced. And, in fact, this strong phototropic response of pea seedlings to blue light is well established in the scientific research literature, and my own pilot study had shown me that pea seedlings were never random in how they directed their growth toward light in the first place.

In other words, unless trained to do otherwise (which was the aim of my experiments), pea seedlings successfully grew in the direction where they last experienced light 100 percent of the time, not a random 50 percent of the time. Plants like peas always grow in the direction of sunlight. How could I miss this vital piece of information, which is so obvious as to be forgotten within the complexities of my experimental groups? This meant that one would never expect them to override their innate tendency to continue growing in the direction of that last-presented light and, instead, use the new direction of the fan (conditioned stimulus) as a reliable indicator of future light. This, and not an imaginary random choice with its expectation of 50:50 being the baseline, was the realistic expectation to measure my results against to observe and recognize whether a learned behavior was being expressed. And by switching the location of the fan after it had been associated with the future presence of light during the learning phase, the study had demonstrated that the green tendrils had done exactly what I had been testing for; between 60 and 70 percent of all peas had learned the association and made a rebellious new choice that was unexpected of them—to turn the other way and go against their instinct of growing where they had last experienced light. And while this provided the mechanistic answer to how the experiment unfolded in the first place, it did little to uncover what provoked the perceptual shift in me—how could I have missed this and then, suddenly, have seen the very thing I was testing for?

I thought I had been waiting for something to happen, and instead I was learning to wait without waiting. I understand now that for the something I was waiting for to appear at all, I had to be willing to be surprised. By definition, of course, a surprise can be possible only if it arrives unannounced, unintended, unpremeditated. The something I was waiting for did appear unanticipated, as the surprise outdid my expectations, based on what I had previously learned. Paradoxically, the very expectations that, at first, concealed the event I was waiting for also provided the essential backdrop against which the event could be seen. My expectations were the background of my knowing within which a kind of inconsistency could be created; they provided the manured topsoil in which the event could emerge from the background to be recognized, making itself available to the eyes and the mind.

By pointing their green tendrils at that which had obscured the possibility of an alternative view, the young peas had created a profound fissure in my well-sculpted perception of the outer world. So as I tested their learning ability within the Pavlovian conditioning paradigm, the seedlings had tested mine by shining a light on the extent to which the conditioning prescribed by my academic training had bound me to a specific perception of the world—one that restricted what I could see. In an act of volition, they had offered themselves as the substrate through which perceptual conditioning could be expressed so that they could show me where my own conditioning lay.

The advent of this recognition had caused me to appreciate the peas (once more) as brilliant collaborators who, by simply growing into what they chose, overthrew—at least in part—the restrictions regimenting my perceptual freedom. This seeing was truly a gift, one that couldn't be lost—once you see, you cannot unsee. It was from this newly found viewpoint that I also understood that the aggression, derision, or cold indifference some colleagues had expressed toward my work over the years had merely been articulations of their visual boundaries. They were unable to see what was presented because it simply did not exist (yet) in their reality—something that, only a moment earlier, had been the case for me too.

This realization arrived with a wonderful sense of freedom, as a more expanded way to perceive both the world and myself opened. As the groundswell of this realization increased over the weeks and months that followed, my field of view stretched farther to consider the wider context of modern human society. Then the big question surfaced—why do we seem so incapable of taking the steps and actions required to create a world where conflict, poverty, and environmental devastation are things of the past? The simplicity and profound wisdom of the answer moved me deeply as it touched the shores of my awareness.

Throughout human history, we have constructed boundaries to define reality in an attempt to soothe our need to feel safe in our own skin and at home in a world we are, fundamentally, so afraid of. Threatening the very thing they promised to protect—our feeling of being safe—these boundaries are, and always were, fictional walls that restrict our understanding of who we truly are and that replace clear seeing with misconception—the illusion that we need to control a world we have no control over. Our need to feel safe (and, correspondingly, the feeling of *not* being safe) in the world seems inextricably linked to our need to control it. But what if we were to realize that the only reason we feel unsafe in the world is because we *believe* we need to control it?

As the sacred jungle Tobacco would teach me a year later, we have no control over the circumstances that face us *until* we surrender the need to control them. As long as we need to control our circumstances, we also need to feel unsafe and insecure about them, because the two states are bound together in a self-perpetuating and irreconcilable loop that goes something like this: we try to control because we feel unsafe and believe that by controlling our world, we will feel safe in it—and yet we never do, and we cannot feel safe in the world if we keep believing that the world needs controlling because, without our control, there is something unsafe about it.

The greatest insanity of this merry-go-round is that the loop we have invented has no possible internal resolution. The anxious feeling of not being safe is a necessary stipulation within our contract with the need to control; with no loophole to be found, we don't know what to do. As I had experienced in my lab when my experiment didn't seem to be working, what if we accepted that there was actually nothing to do? And once faced with this dead end, what if we stopped and waited in the darkness, like I had to on that Sunday morning? And as we relaxed in the belly of the unknown and handed ourselves over to life, what if we discovered a surprising clarity to *see* what is truly happening and what needs to be done? By dropping our obsession for controlling life, the whole fiction about "being unsafe" drops too. Left with nothing to protect or attack, the loop comes undone!

It seems our society is ready for a perceptual shift capable of undoing this silly loop by overthrowing our conditioned seeing, ready for a disobedient disruption emerging from the tidy background of silent obligations and prepackaged reality that have prevented us from seeing the innovative solutions that could bring planetary well-being and peace into being. The walls that entrap us in the loop are not as impenetrable as we believe. Porous, precarious, and of disputable nature, they were designed to dissolve at the first pure moment of real surrender!

Just like I had experienced with my clever peas in the darkness of my lab, it is when we are willing to let life surprise us that alternatives and unanticipated solutions become visible and accessible. And the best part of this entire process is that once out of our insane loop of control and insecurity, we are effortlessly delivered exactly where we are going. Infused with a sense of awe and deep trust in the life that we are, we wait without waiting to know exactly what to do and when. Free to see clearly, we don't need to find our way out of the maze. We realize there never was a maze.

Chapter H

True leadership gives space.

~ As Above, So Below ~

Hidden in plain sight, continuities elude us. Unnoticed threads that endure throughout the fabric of the universe, continuities ambush our tenacious proclivity to split the world in one or another version of itself, so that perceived polarities may be reconciled. By dispelling the myth of polarities, continuities release us from the unbearable, but needed, tension involved in having to make choices between absurd opposites. This tension is needed as a constant invitation to sense the presence of a glitch in our perception. Once this glitch is seen, continuities can deliver us right in the middle of an unnameable emptiness, where all polarities cease to exist, as they arise into the manifestation of each other. And it is by experiencing this paradox that we arrive in the middle. The middle—despite the common use of that word—is not halfway between here and there, beginning and end, birth and death, right and wrong. The middle is no place at all, but an undecided space that lingers between our illusion of polarities, containing them both and being empty of both, at once uniting and separating. Here we see it all, at last. Here and now we are free, at last.

To this day, I find it difficult to grasp what powered the gestalt shift I experienced in my lab that Sunday. Was it the pea who made it happen, or was I solely responsible, or were we both? Did the plant intend to surprise the human, or was it the human who intended to be surprised? All I knew was that both the plant and the human were involved in the creative process of the scientific investigation; both made themselves available to encounter and act on the other, and as a result, they transformed one another. In doing so—together—they unsettled the belief that there is an edge that truly separates one from the other. And sitting on that illusory edge, I felt the otherworldly grin of an amused Ayahuma. With exquisite precision, she had set in motion the circumstances that unfolded into a profound demonstration that what we see is what we are accustomed to seeing and that the reality we perceive is composed of a narrow set of familiar things and contexts we feel at home with. In the study with the peas learning in the maze, the step beyond the comfort of these habituated scenes was heralded by a state of unsettling confusion, a necessary feeling of discomfort that, unsurprisingly, I tried to avoid until the unexpected arrived in my field of perception. And what an incredible experience it was!

As the sense of marvel for the process I experienced started to arise, so was my mind already seizing ideas to explain how it all happened and turning it all into something "known"—therein laying the trap, as any landmark used to delineate the boundaries of material reality keeps you fixated. Any thought pattern that solidifies the construct ensnares you. Of course, I was not aware of any of this until much later.[1] At the time, I was simply moving back and forth between the cold darkness of the controlled-environment room, where the Pavlovian pea experiment was progressing silently, and the sunny brightness of a small greenhouse, where another experiment with pea plants and sound was taking shape, implemented according to a second set of instructions and diagrams Ayahuma had imparted during the *dieta* in the Peruvian jungle.

I remember it well. On the second-to-last day of my *dieta* with the mighty Ayahuma tree, a question arrived—can plant roots find water by means of acoustic vibrations? Impressed on the page of my travel diary, the blue-inked scribble was accompanied by a diagram similar to the one Ayahuma had me sketch for the Pavlovian pea experiment, except that the whole affair was now turned on its head. Sometimes the only way to see circumstances differently and perceive alternate possibilities is to turn them upside down. Of course, the notion that plants could be using sound to locate vital resources such as water was not new to me; I had discussed this possibility with my colleagues at the University in Bristol, where I had measured the vegetal clicks emitted by yellow kernels of corn. However, I had formulated no experimental approach for testing it, and now Ayahuma was inviting me to explore this question: "You need to give space for a free choice to be possible." The reader will not be surprised now to know that, upon my return to Australia, I promptly secured one of the greenhouses within the Plant Growth Facilities at the university campus and converted it into my plant acoustic behavioral laboratory to start the new research project.[2]

The small rectangular greenhouse was warm and sunny. It was temperature-regulated by ventilation fans and automated shade-screening systems controlled by sensors and temperature probes. Along three of its glass walls, there were simple, sturdy wooden benches upon which, at any one time, dozens of inverted Y-shaped mazes paraded like a formation of headless soldiers in white uniforms and black boots (Figure 5). Constructed out of white PVC pipe, each maze was filled with soil, and two tightly fitting black plastic pots were attached at each lower end. Each maze housed a single pea seedling, planted at the top and left to grow undisturbed in the sunny greenhouse. To me, greenhouses are interesting but also strangely disturbing places. Greenhouses were first used to house exotic tropical plants requiring winter protection back in Roman times and then employed to shelter precious orange and lemon trees imported from the Far East to Europe during the late Middle Ages and onward. The concept of the greenhouse as a place devoted to the care and protection of plants has certainly enjoyed a good reputation across the centuries.[3]

Despite the transparency of its walls, however, the greenhouse has also sheltered ideologies of elitism, protecting the complex mélange of power, knowledge, and wealth represented by exotic plants. And it continues to be an emblem of a privileged social status enabled by knowledge and secured through economic profits. Greenhouses today—whether standing in the world's most famous botanical gardens and at educational and research institutions like the university where I worked or dedicated to the intensive production systems of the agroindustry—are still devoted to complex biopolitical agendas. Evocative of colonialist approaches of subjugation and oppression, they continue perpetuating the objectification of plants as pure commodities within a capitalistic model of production and consumption.[4]

Poignantly, etched in the word *greenhouse* is also the expression of our current environmental anxiety and biopolitical dispute concerning global warming. In spite of vested interests paying to discredit the unequivocal message of climate scientists and sponsoring meager excuses over the necessity for immediate action, the fact is obvious. The same system essential to supporting all life on the planet—the Earth's *natural* greenhouse effect, whereby the atmosphere traps enough heat to keep the entire planet nice and cozy in a way similar to the warming process inside a greenhouse—is now threatening us all. This is due to the unprecedented high concentrations of greenhouse gases in the atmosphere caused by humanity's burning of fossil fuels and clearing of forests, revealing the recalcitrant, delusional nature of a capitalistic modus operandi. While we were busy domesticating plants of all kinds and from all places in the pretentious environment of European greenhouses, we avoided noticing that we were fashioning a greenhouse of planetary proportions. It was invisible at first. Then its glass door started rattling on its hinges, warning us through a myriad of ways. The noise grew louder. That door is now ready to close, locking us and all life on Earth in a deadly stalemate—unless we are willing to face the choice we seem to consistently avoid.

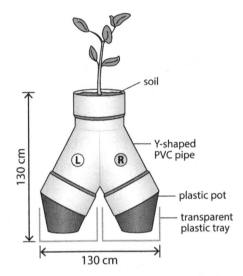

Figure 5. Schematic representation of the custom-designed experimental Y-maze (not in scale). The experimental Y-maze was made of a PVC pipe filled with soil and attached to two tightly fitting small black plastic pots and two transparent rectangular plastic trays at each lower end. Figure reproduced from: M. Gagliano, M. Grimonprez, M. Depczynski, and M. Renton, "Tuned In: Plant Roots Use Sound to Locate Water," Oecologia 184 (2017): 151–160.

Our capacity and willingness to make good choices and sound decisions is not hardwired in our genes; it is a learned skill, and plants can be great teachers. They know that there is no one-size-fits-all solution to a challenge; they know that diversity and acceptance of the other are the keys to any successful survival strategy; they know that an all-embracing approach allows for different possibilities to emerge and merge into remarkable, even surprising, ways of solving a problem. Let me explain through my experiments.

Hidden like clever new ideas snuggled under the surface of the rich soil that would support their growth, the young peas were quietly growing in their mazes in the airy greenhouse. On the surface, nothing happened for a few days. Then out of nowhere, a splash of brilliant green burst out of the dark soil and a leafy shoot materialized, seemingly unforeseen. By then, below the surface, the young pea roots had already made a start on their adventurous journey inside the maze's darkness. Elongating their roots through the soil by the exclusive movement of their expert spearheading tips,[5] exploring this way or that way and constantly making a myriad of choices about where to go, when to go, and how quickly to go, while barely knowing enough about their circumstances, the seedlings were on a mission to find their holy grail—water. It is well known that the roots of plants can "sniff" water's presence by using moisture gradients, but what happens when the moisture gradient is not close enough to be detected? How do plants know the best direction to turn to find water? Following Ayahuma's instructions, I had set up a series of experiments that would answer these questions and open a new scientific vista onto the vegetal realm.

In general, organisms use various kinds of information transmitted by smells, sounds, lights, or magnetic fields in order to make good choices and avoid fatal errors. Based on this idea and as instructed by Ayahuma, I designed the experiments with the peas in the maze to test how roots choose the direction that correctly leads them to water, depending on the cues available. Particularly, could the roots of the young peas sense the acoustic vibrations generated by water moving underground or inside pipes? Could they use the sound of water alone to detect and find its source, when no actual water was available in close vicinity?

To answer this, I wrapped a sealed, soft plastic pipe through which water was constantly flowing around the base of one side of the maze, but the water itself was never directly accessible to the plants. Then I compared the choices roots made in these mazes to those they made growing in mazes where the soil was kept moist by actual water contained in the small plastic tray attached at the base of one side of the maze, hence producing a moisture gradient.

What emerged was exciting. In mazes in which actual water was available, the vast majority of seedlings followed the moisture gradient and directed their root to the side where the water source was located. But seedlings were equally successful at locating the water source when they grew in mazes in which they had no direct access to water—no moisture gradient—but only the sound of water circulating inside the sealed pipes. And if both a moisture gradient and the sound of water were made available in the same maze, what would the young plants choose? They chose the obvious—with no hesitation, the vast majority of seedlings grew their roots into the side of the upside-down Y-maze that led them straight to water! While moisture or acoustic cues are equally useful in helping roots locate water, their relevance and usefulness to a plant depend on the context. What the peas were really showing me was that they choose which cue is most advantageous in what circumstance.

From this perspective, my ecological and logical interpretation was that sound may enable peas to roughly detect the presence of water at a distance and, conceivably, to establish the most direct and sensible route to that source before any soil moisture is encountered. An analogy might be a bubbling watercourse in the distance or water coursing through underground fissures. Once accessible, however, it is the moisture gradient in the soil that helps them home in on their target more accurately and pinpoint the exact location of the water source. Clearly, the sensory world of plants contains a more complex assortment of informational components than what I had presented them with and, as they would show me next, they are extremely good at resolving an enormous influx of information by prioritizing cues that support the overall most beneficial decision.

The next step in my research was to establish whether the peas were really responding to the sound of water or were simply growing toward any source of noise regardless of what the nature of the sound actually was. This was important to see just how selective and attuned they were to an ecologically relevant and rewarding sound. In animal ecology, this question is commonly addressed by playback experiments, a widely used technique in which natural or synthetic acoustic stimuli are broadcast and the response of individuals noted. I applied this approach to the young peas and found something that, at first, puzzled me—the seedlings directed their roots *away* from the recorded sound of water. I had attached a vibration speaker directly to one of the black plastic pots at the base of the maze. The speaker was then connected to a small MP3 player, which played the recorded sound of water in some mazes or broadcast either computer-generated white noise or silence in others. Regardless of the sound treatment I applied, none of the seedlings had access to actual water. What I found was that the majority of seedlings grew away from the side of the maze where I had attached the sound equipment, regardless of the sound playing. In fact, they avoided that side of the maze even when I played them silence! It seemed as if the seedlings were repelled by the speakers themselves. Because speakers contain small magnets, and plants are known to orientate their root systems in response to natural magnetic fields (such as gravity) as well as artificial ones, I started to suspect that perhaps the sound equipment emitted a electromagnetic (EM) field that, while imperceptible to me, was tangible enough to be sensed and avoided by the young roots.

I excitedly emailed the school of physics that housed the BioMagnetics research group, a specialized lab equipped with state-of-the-art magnetic measurement facilities to investigate the role of magnetism in biological systems, explaining that I was conducting some greenhouse experiments on the acoustic abilities of plants and that I had just stumbled onto something potentially interesting: "I think my peas are sensing the EM field emitted by my sound equipment." It was April 2. A couple of days later, I received a reply that opened, "Hi Monica, to be honest, if I got your email a day earlier I would have just thought it was a April Fools joke."

Although I discovered later that measuring EM emissions was not particularly hard, I waited for four months for my colleague to take a look at the speakers and MP3 players, as he had agreed to do. The task remained on his permanent to-do list, and after too many broken promises and countless postponements, I decided to improvise. I equipped myself with a portable low-frequency analyzer (or gaussmeter), and off I went. I measured the magnetic emissions from the sound equipment when it was turned off and compared it with the readings made when the sound equipment was turned on and playing any of the sounds I had used in the experiment with the peas. And what a surprise! When turned on, the sound equipment (the speakers and MP3 player) did produce measureable levels of magnetic emissions that could be detected within a five-centimeter radius around the source—this range happened to correspond almost exactly to the dimensions of the black plastic pot the speaker was attached to, thus making a highly localized disturbance obvious at one foot of the maze.

Trivial from a human perspective, the range of influence was absolutely relevant to the roots in the space they occupied inside the maze, and they had demonstrated this accordingly through their behavior. This was a brilliant find, of course, but the disturbing influence of the magnetic field emitted by the sound equipment now posed an unexpected complication in my attempt to discover whether roots responded selectively to the sound of water. Or so it seemed. Over the years, I had learned that seemingly problematic issues that materialize unpredictably and demand a change in existing plans can feel frustrating, but they often bear immensely productive insights and opportunities if I am prepared to stay open to alternatives. So after putting up with some initial frustration, I moved into the next phase of the research and presented the seedlings with a new choice—one between the monsters Scylla and Charybdis, so to speak.

On their epic journey through the maze, the pea seedlings reminded me of Odysseus, who, in Homer's *Odyssey,* had to negotiate his memorable passage between the deadly clutches of Scylla and Charybdis, the two immortal monsters inhabiting either side of a narrow strait.[6] In this new phase of the research, the young plants, like the Homeric hero, were to face a choice between two evils. I attached a speaker and MP3 player to each foot of the maze, one side playing the sound of water and the other side playing either white noise or silence—thus experimentally standardizing the strong repulsive effect of the sound equipment. Now that the magnetic interference was originating from both sides of the maze and could not be avoided, could the peas face what they were avoiding and choose what was most needed, namely water?

Caught between two equally unpleasant alternatives, the peas did exactly what was most appropriate, given the circumstances. Availing themselves of the other cues present in their immediate environment, the vast majority of seedlings extended their roots toward the recorded sound of water, when the player on the other side of the maze was broadcasting silence. The preference was not as strong when the other side broadcast white noise, but the recorded sound of water was still more attractive than the white noise.

Of course, this confirmed that plants preferentially moved toward the sound of water, a previously unknown phenomenon, and yet this finding of their "hearing" abilities should not come as a surprise. Over their evolutionary history, plants would have had millennia to evolve this ability to listen to and discriminate between vibrations of various kinds and then respond to those sounds that carried some meaning to them. For example, sounds produced by a running stream would have been highly relevant to a broad range of plant species and beneficial to their survival. Similarly, it was not totally surprising to see that the ability of the seedlings to clearly detect the recorded sound of water was somewhat reduced by the presence of white noise. The two sounds would have bumped into each other inside the maze, resulting in acoustic interference.

This kind of masking effect has been observed in animal systems. From studies of birds, bats, and squirrels, to name a few, we know that white noise can interfere with an animal's ability to receive and respond to particular relevant sounds and, consequently, can make it trickier for the animal to carry on everyday business effectively. What was striking about this finding, however, was that we had never before considered the possibility that human-altered soundscapes and acoustic pollution could be issues of potentially vital importance to plants.

By prioritizing cues that supported growth, the peas spoke of *responsibility*. "Responsibility is that which you are moving toward," the plants have told me. "It is not a moral obligation, but rather the actual movement that supports the expression of care." Inside the maze, the young pea roots had revealed an unwavering commitment to making the choice that nurtures and supports life—in this case, by finding water. "We are both living on the same earth, and we are both after the same water," they have said.

In making their choices, the young plants were also reiterating the fundamental fact that we, humans, need the same things to flourish as plants and all life on the planet. We all have the same choices to make, choices that concern the well-being of the whole. And, ultimately, *all* choices are inescapably about the well-being of the whole; they differ only in the quality of their movement—some move us all toward a state of planetary vitality and health, and some away from it. Just the same, they carry us all inexorably toward the circumstances that we sow, and therefore, it seems essential to care for what is planted.

It is, then, the quality of our actions that tells the story of who we are and where we are going. Unfortunately, many of our current actions are violent, and we are living in the delusion that we can distance and guard ourselves from their consequences, as if our well-being is separate from that of the whole. Well, we cannot. We cannot because the notion that there are independent objects, each fighting for dear life in a Darwinian struggle of existence, is a lazy and archaic conjecture that does not do justice to contemporary scientific findings. There are no conflicting opponents, even when two organisms appear to have mutually exclusive properties;[7] there is only the remarkable play of one nature displayed across a palette of rainbow colors. However, until we see ourselves inhabiting a world of polarities, we can only perceive ourselves in conflict with the whole—and our neurotic violence keeps chasing and biting at our own figurative tail.

From this partial perspective, it is inevitable that the fact that our well-being is inseparable from environmental integrity generates such an unbearable tension in our society. We approach this tension by making violence permissible, so that we may justify actions that are carrying the whole to where no one actually wants to go. Instead, we should resolve our core blindness, acquiring the lucidity to see that the dynamic movement of existence is a fundamental state of communion and, hence, acting in ways that can only be beneficial to the whole—existence itself. We can opt for a reality woven together by the threads of continuity or endure the illusory belief that the world is split into an interminable succession of polarities and keep facing conflicting, even paradoxical, circumstances. This does not need to be, and choices that seem contradictory need not be so either.

To make some sense of this, I had to go back to the peas in the maze. By moving away from the sound of water emanating from a speaker at one foot of the maze, the peas in my experiment made what seemed an incongruous choice—plants surely want water no matter what, so why move away from the sound of it? As if knowing more than the appearances alluded to, the young peas made the choice that was required and moved away from trouble by, somewhat, staying at it! In the scenario they found themselves in, they selected to avoid the disturbing, possibly damaging, effects of the magnetic field produced by the sound equipment, even if that meant moving away from what was desired, namely water. In order to keep themselves safe from the harm of magnetic disturbance, they accepted the fact that water had to be found elsewhere or in some other way.

Paradoxically, the peas had made the most appropriate choice—if they had grown their roots toward the sound of water, they would have found *only* the magnetic disturbance and no actual water. In other words, the young plants selected something that may not be immediately beneficial but ultimately gives them a better chance of survival, rather than choosing what seemed to provide the desirable outcome, despite its disastrous consequences. By attending to what was asked by the circumstances with *responsibility,* the peas had effectively moved toward that which supports and protects care in the long run.

To me, the peas' behavior inside the maze was a great lesson in the kind of responsibility the plants had spoken of to me earlier—ultimately, a choice is as good as the level of integrity we can bring to it, and it is integrity within the actions that reveals us and that ultimately defines us. Are we able to make the choice that is required and move away from our global environmental crisis by standing for what we must? Human prosperity is not in conflict with the prosperity of other species and the planet; on the contrary, thriving abundance is *made-with,*[8] cocreated with others in a continuity of exchanges and sharings. In this continuity, we have no conflict to resolve and no riddle to be solved. We only have choices to make.

Like the peas in the maze, can we move away from what injures, even if this means moving away from what we *think* is most wanted? In order to keep the Earth and all her living species (including ourselves) safe from the threats posed by environmental deterioration, climate change, and mass extinction, are we able to accept the fact that human behavior has to find other ways of being? The faulty thinking stopping us from making the most appropriate choice is prolonging our destructive impact on the planet and, hence, ensuring that we may experience *only* conflict and destruction. At this crucial juncture in the evolutionary history of the planet and all living species, the circumstances are asking us to dream ourselves beyond the discordant format of a polarized reality and forward to more supportive futures.

Just like the peas in the maze, it is our conduct toward releasing the knot of the current eco-cultural tangle that reveals us in the end. And while the deafening sound of too many words still echoes between here and there, right and wrong, from life to death and back again, it is in the silent quality of our actions that the genuine spirit and kind heart of humanity is revealed. And it is then when alternate possibilities, which seem too far off, become so close; from the space in the middle, these choices are separated by only a thin pane of glass.

Chapter A

No more dreaming with your eyes closed.
Open your eyes.
You are dreaming.

~ Being in Time and Space ~

All the stories we tell seem to start long ago in some faraway place. Like a beacon of inspiration, they are the voice that reminds us of the place we are going to by showing us that we have already arrived. The path unfolds as a remembrance of itself, forward to the beginning, a point of origin where all timelines and dreamscapes join, dissolve, unify. When we truly understand that nothing really ends and nothing really begins, we transcend the story, all of the stories we tell of ourselves. When we clearly see the very nothing we have been pursuing far and wide, we arrive. This nothingness contains all the beauty and horror of our stories, which emerge as the dream we are having. And yet, intrinsically, nothing happens.

The familiar sound of the kettle coming to the boil temporarily interrupted our conversation. I got up from my chair, went to the kitchen, and poured the hot water in the two cups that were waiting on the bench top. Within seconds, the aromas of the flowers and leaves contained inside the tea bags wafted out of each cup and free into the room. Holding one cup in each hand, I walked back to the lounge and resumed my chin-wag with Valerie, an incredibly gifted sound healer as well as a professional writer. I had met her in passing several years earlier in Perth, where she had come from San Francisco to visit her brother, my next-door neighbor at the time. While that first meeting was brief and somewhat accidental, it was the seed of a friendship that has kept growing over time, despite the distance between us. Every time I found myself in the San Francisco Bay Area, we would meet, and sometimes I would stay at her house. Even when years had gone by since we'd last seen each other, it was as if we had just caught up the previous day. Like all other times, we were once again sitting in the lounge with a cup of tea, updating one another on our respective lives. And, like all other times, we knew that our converging was the harbinger of some bizarre but usually amazing adventure coming our way. And curious things did start to happen during that visit.

It was October 2014. I had come to the United States to speak at a number of conferences, including the twenty-fifth National Bioneers Conference held in San Rafael, a little place across the Golden Gate Bridge from San Francisco and (most excitingly for me) a short drive to Mount Tamalpais, home to *Sequoia sempervirens,*[1] the giant coast redwoods at the Muir Woods National Monument. Throughout my visit, I had met some truly inspiring human beings and felt deeply touched and expanded by those encounters. I had also had the precious opportunity to share my own work with a large number of people and excite (at least, some of) them about what I called the *real* plant revolution[2] that was taking place in science.

The adjective *real* was to distinguish it from its homonym—a plant revolution, also know as the "green revolution," which spoke of the glory of plant biotechnology and the many achievements and benefits of plant engineering and its capacity to deliver healthier foods and, most crucially, contribute to global food security.[3] *That* plant revolution spoke of an ever-increasing investment in research and development for the making of transgenic plants to be *used* as highly profitable objects of insatiable financial interests. Far from being original or revolutionary, that plant revolution had succeeded in investing considerably in brains, money, and technology so that an outmoded and erroneous story—a story that was, in fact, thousands of years old—could be recited over and over again and sanctioned as scientific research. And by simply doing so, that story has now grown into a serious business with huge power. Because stories are never *just* stories, the stories we tell come to describe the way we shape and move in the world. Of course, we can choose whatever story we want, but given that stories frame what beliefs we elect to embody and which path we choose to walk on for our becoming as individuals and society, shouldn't we be extremely observant and mindful of the stories we tell and subscribe to?

The story that cemented the foundation for *that* plant revolution dates back to Aristotle, perhaps the most influential thinker of all of Western history. By defining insensitivity as the key criterion to differentiate plants from animals (including human beings) and hence positioning plants outside of the domain of sensitive life, the Aristotelian story had, in effect, transformed plants into objects—a spurious idea that still sanctions the human right to use (and abuse) plants and that exempts us from any sense of responsibility or respect toward them as living beings.

Aristotle's perspective of the sensorial world had a profound and long-lasting influence on virtually everyone who came after him, beginning with his own pupil Theophrastus, who, despite his own observations of active behaviors in many different plant species, blindly subscribed to the Aristotelian belief of plant passivity and insensitivity.[4] Over the millennia, this story accrued such power that we have come to accept it as truth and, most dangerously, to glorify the approach of sameness and uniformity that it preaches. As its unquestioning devotees, we act in the world as if such uniformity is a truth rather than a silly fib. And worst, we are untroubled by our readiness to overlook our own incongruity, when we teach our undergraduate students to appreciate that nature thrives on variation and diversity and that the existence of such variation among individuals and the mortality of individuals based on this variation are the fundamental principles of the Darwinian theory of natural selection. We know very well that greater species diversity, both in terms of actual numbers and the genetic variation within species, ensures greater ecosystem stability. In turn, healthier ecosystems are more resilient to stress and can better withstand and recover from adverse conditions.

Similarly, we are equally aware that modern industrialized agricultural practices focused on the regimented monoculture of uniform crops lead to unstable agro-ecosystems by selectively reducing both the genetic and the phenotypic variability of those plant species. By constraining them as obligate annuals[5] designed for uninhibited sex and early death, the process of converting wild species into tamed plants fit for human consumption has enfeebled them, stripping them of their ability to communicate effectively to protect themselves from pests and diseases.[6] The plant biotechnology story clearly is a poor choice. The good news is that this is not the only available narrative that science can offer.

The other, parallel story enlivened by recent scientific research is, in fact, quite different, in that it reminds us of how plants themselves constantly share their personal stories with us through shapes, colors, smells, sounds, and astonishing behavioral choices.[7] In doing so, they are already inspiring us to reenvision the world and assisting us in building the future and a new way forward for human societies. This is the *real* plant revolution. In this story, plants show no sign of being insensitive object-like organisms. In fact, the fast-accruing evidence from scientific research is a confirmation of the polar opposite. It is clear, then, that condemning plants to the insensitive realm à la Aristotle is perverse, in the least, and surely no longer scientifically defensible, given its false premise. Indeed, the chief characteristic that distinguishes the scientific method from other methods of exploring and acquiring knowledge about the world around us is its unwavering pledge to let reality speak for itself. Appropriately, a theory is supported when its predictions are confirmed by our observations of reality, and it is challenged, rectified, or even rejected when its predictions prove to be false, no matter how old and beloved that theory is. So the question that emerges is this: how can we justify, promote, and financially subsidize the use of plants in biotechnology and bioengineering[8] when the premises of this scientific endeavor are rooted in the erroneous view of plants as insensitive organisms?[9]

The development of plant bioengineering, particularly genetically modified (GM) plant research, is an emotionally charged and highly politicized and polarized issue in our society, but the growing plethora of scientific evidence demonstrating that plants are highly sensitive living organisms can offer a detached and unequivocally clear resolution to a much-heated issue. Our current scientific knowledge allows us to appreciate plants as sovereign *subjects* of their own lives rather than usable *objects* of ours. This makes the Aristotelian proposition of plants invalid. It also shows that GM plant research has been inaccurately presented as a scientific practice, given that its premise—the use of plants as inert objects, made by humans for entirely human purposes—is unsupported by modern scientific evidence (that plants are living subjects, pursuing their own raison de vivre of being themselves).[10] Under these circumstances, the scientific method demands us to rectify our approach by de-objectifying plants and no longer granting scientific legitimacy to GM plant research.

At a time when modern society relies on its scientific prowess to provide answers and, ideally, solutions for the current socio-environmental crisis, applying the scientific method with the uttermost integrity is not optional. Failing to integrate new knowledge and scientific evidence and correct or, when appropriate, reject old beliefs is what defines pseudoscience—theories and beliefs that are regarded as scientific facts but lack controlled experimental evidence carefully collected by appropriate scientific methods. No scientist truly committed to science would want to be accused of practicing pseudoscience, so why should taxpayers' money be used to support it?

By the time my 2014 visit in the United States was coming to a close, I felt the kind of contentment that one experiences after a lush, soul-nourishing meal shared with friends. With only a few days left in the country before returning down under, I had two things I really wanted to do—first, meet "the Diviner," a man my friend Valerie had told me about and, second, pay a visit to the redwood trees in the Muir Woods as my way of giving thanks for the incredibly fulfilling time and amazing trip I had had in their homeland (once again). Little did I know that a few days were ample time for both of these meetings to take place, as well as for a most bizarre and peculiar series of events, magical occurrences arising from these two encounters—with the Diviner and the redwood trees, who would deliver the proverbial cherry on top of the ice cream sundae I had just started savoring.

The Diviner was a tall man with a welcoming demeanor. He spent several years in training with the Dagara people of West Africa, who taught him about their divination system—specifically, voice divination—so he could assist people in reconnecting with themselves, nature, and the spirit world. I had no idea what voice divination was or what I had signed up for by coming to this meeting.

Now, sitting on the floor of a tiny room in front of a small altar that was covered with a wide variety of objects—a strange and random-looking assortment of small shells, wooden sticks, pebbles, and tiny pieces of metal—I was taken aback in utter bewilderment as the divination began. The Diviner put on a peculiar outfit—a loose-fitting, embroidered ritual robe that draped down to his feet, beaded regalia that crowned his head, and a mask over his face—and with a rattling stick in one hand, he disappeared inside a curtained booth set up in a corner of the small room. Nothing happened for a minute or so. Then, from inside the booth, he started speaking in a hilariously high-pitched and squeaky voice, the kind of sound one makes after inhaling helium. I turned to look at Valerie, who had stayed in the room and was sitting right behind me. I can't even start imagining the look I must have had on my face—I was ready to burst into irreverent laughter, and I could not believe what was happening.

Everything seemed so surreal, and yet, as I turned back to look in front of me at the altar with all its odd objects, I felt sincere appreciation for the deep sacredness and heartfelt devotion the whole situation entailed. As a voice diviner, the Diviner performed the ritual by channeling the Kontomblé—which is the name given by the Dagara people to inter-dimensional beings such as elementals and nature spirits, otherwise known as fairies, elves, and gnomes. To achieve this, he had learned to merge with the Kontomblé, allowing his body to become a channel through which the Kontomblé communicated cryptic messages, which the Diviner would later interpret. Basically, I was witnessing a spirit possession, and be assured, this was to be no monologue—I was to be an active participant in the whole affair. At times, the squeaky voice would speak to the Diviner, while at other times, it would speak directly to me, asking specific and personal questions—"personal" in the sense that the questions related to weird and wonderful encounters and experiences I had had with animals, plants, and places in nature, which no one necessarily knew about.

By the time the divination ended, I had been assigned a list of nine personal rituals to be completed within a year's time, which included offerings of water, ash, and milk designed to honor the spirits that supported my growth and my understanding of the nature of nature and the nature of reality. As we walked out of the room, I felt unable to say anything. As powerful as it was, it is what happened once we left the Diviner and drove back to Valerie's place that made the whole experience of monumental consequence.

The drive was the perfect time to debrief on what had just happened. As Valerie drove, I started reading out loud the list of rituals I had to perform. We quickly realized that some rituals were pretty straightforward and would be relatively easy to accomplish, while others seemed more challenging. This is when we started discussing the issue of the gold ring. You see—one of the rituals the Kontomblé had asked me to perform involved a gold ring, which I was to offer to my mother. According to the Kontomblé, this would clear all negativity in my relationship with her within this current timeline, and it would cleanse our relationship of any hostility, pain, distrust, and abuse that had been stored within the ancestral feminine line that had birthed us both and of which I was one of its latest member. Fabulous!

But here the first obstacle appeared. Aside from the fact that I see my mother only every few years, as we live on opposite sides of the world, I never liked gold and owned not one single piece of gold, let alone a gold ring. So how and when was I supposed to fulfill this ritual request? As we continued deliberating on the situation, Valerie made an astonishing offer. "If you really think about it," she said, "there is one ancestral source from which all women have come forth." She stopped at an intersection, as the traffic light turn red, and then continued, "while you perform this ritual to clear your line, you naturally also clear part of my line and those of all women." She waited for the traffic light to turned green and then said, "I have the gold ring you need." She paused for a minute, as she searched in her mind. "When we get home, I will check if it still is where I think it is." And with the satisfied smile of someone who had just solved a most intricate brainteaser, she added, "The ring was a gift to me from my mother."

The next day, I traveled very light for my brief trip to the Muir Woods National Monument. In my backpack, I carried a drinking bottle full of water and a Peruvian drawstring pouch, a hand-woven bag small enough to be unobtrusive but big enough for the essentials for a little ritual. On my way to the redwoods, I stopped by Valerie's house for a quick hello. This is when she gave me the gold ring, which I placed inside the ritual pouch for safekeeping. "Do you want to take this with you today?" She held out a blue pendant ocarina—a simple, flute-like wind instrument made of glazed terracotta. "Brilliant idea!" I replied, "I may play it for the trees." I thanked her for the loan, which I squeezed into the little space left inside my ritual pouch, and headed off, buzzing and elated.

My excitement, which accompanied me all the way to the entrance to the Muir Woods, was suddenly killed at the disturbing sight of what—to me—looked like an ocean of huge charter coaches crammed side by side in the parking area. What was I really thinking—that I would have the forest all to myself, quiet and undisturbed? Of course it would be full of tourists. They were moving in amorphous herds, voices blaring and taking photos with their smartphones, under the watch of their keeper, who would wave the right colored flag or call them in the right language to keep them somehow all gathered together to direct their attention this or that way. I was horrified.

This was certainly not what I had in mind—and just as well, because I was about to discover that this visit had really nothing at all to do with my mind. I parked, got out of my rental car, and started walking at a brisk pace toward the visitor center, where I found a gift shop, a café, a booth with useful information on which trails to explore and points of interest to check out, and of course, my entry ticket. Surprisingly, despite the crowd, there was no queue at the ticket booth. Within no time, I had paid my entrance fee, and I was on the Redwood Creek Trail, walking in the forest and discovering something absurd that I had not even considered until that moment—the crowd seemed to be mostly interested in the gift shop and the café. So the deeper one walked into the forest and away from those amenities, the quieter, more private and pleasant it all became. How can anyone really see the forest, truly hear the whispers of those ancient trees with all that noise? As I walked farther along the trail, I found myself coming across fewer and fewer people, and I felt happy.

I had been walking for only a brief while when the main trail branched into two options. One arrow pointed the direction for a longer hike to Camp Alice Eastwood and beyond, while the other signaled the way to a shorter and possibly easier walk along the Fern Creek Trail. Before choosing which way to go, I sat on a big boulder close to the bifurcation. A few people passed by and greeted me quietly or simply nodded. I took a sip of water and considered how much time I had for my walk.

As I sat there, I felt the need to take my boots and socks off to feel the earth under my bare soles. My feet were firmly on the ground when a third option made itself available—a small trail running off to the other side of Redwood Creek. The path was not marked by any arrow or sign I could see, but it was definitely beckoning me to it, so the choice was made. I walked across a narrow bridge that had been built atop a large fallen redwood—a tree who, at a much earlier time perhaps, had made itself conveniently available as the original bridge for crossing over the creek. Soon I found myself moving along a narrow dirt path cut into the side of a hill. The width of a single person, the trail was incredibly quiet and peaceful. I paused, inhaled deeply, and smiled at the silent realization that no human voices were audible from here. I listened to the bright sound of the birds and the loud stillness of the giants that surrounded me. Inside, I was giggling like a child, and without warning, that child came out to play for a few seconds when my bare feet splashed in the shallow waters of a muddy puddle that had formed right across the path I was on. With wet feet and a feeling of great contentment in my heart, I kept walking, and as the light filtered through the high canopy of the redwoods to illuminate different fragments of ferny greens and red-brown barks down below, I saw the perfect spot for my thanksgiving ritual. I approached the tree that felt just right for the occasion and sat at its feet.

Out of my drawstring pouch came the blue ocarina, a piece of clear quartz, sacred tobacco leaves, and a lock of my hair, which for no particular reason, I had decided to keep after cutting my hair a few weeks earlier. Using a short twig, I drew a small circle in the soft dirt right in front of where I was sitting, sprinkled some tobacco as my offering to the place and then positioned the quartz in front of me on the line that demarcated my impromptu thanksgiving altar. In the middle of the circle, I dug a bowl-shaped depression, and inside this simple receptacle I placed some more tobacco and the lock of hair. Then, suddenly, I understood. There was one more thing that needed to be offered for this ritual, and my hand went back inside my drawstring pouch and feverishly searched for it—the gold ring. The Kontomblé had asked me to offer a gold ring to my mother. Only in that moment, though, did I realize which mother it had been referring to. As it lay down in its earthy cradle lined with hair and tobacco, the ring shined, and something felt extremely right. I knew the whole forest was quietly witnessing what was taking place, and to this unobtrusive but comforting audience, I started playing the ocarina. I should clarify that I had had a go at playing this instrument before, and the sounds I had been able to produce had always been kind of annoying, high-pitched shrieks. In the woods, however, clear, bright tones soared out of the little flute like tiny sky-blue birds, and I too became the audience; I too listened deeply and unobtrusively to the call of one heart that sung for everyone, that belongs to everyone. In that moment, when the whole is able to witness itself being, the bewitching spell of time and space is no longer required.

When the ocarina stopped playing, all that remained was an inexplicably absolute silence—no rumblings and grumblings of the water in the creek below or the wind high in the canopy, no twittering and chirping of birds or insects, no voices at all—not even the sound of a leaf dropping to the ground. I didn't dare move. I soaked in the silence, and then I knew my thanksgiving ritual was complete. I covered the offerings with dirt and compacted the ground over the space to leave no sign of the depression I had made. The clear quartz returned into the drawstring pouch, together with the ocarina, and I gently rubbed away the circle I had drawn. All that was left as a reminder of the preciousness that had just occurred there was the maroon underbelly of a heart-shaped leaf I had collected earlier along the path—a leaf that belonged to the delicate redwood sorrel, the clover-looking plant that carpeted the forest floor.

I had no idea how long I had been there; it didn't matter. Finally, I stood up and hesitated for a moment, pondering which direction to take. On the one hand, I wanted to walk the Fern Creek Trail, which linked up to Lost Trail, and to do that, I had to go back the same way I had come and return to the bifurcation on the other side of the creek. On the other hand, the narrow dirt trail I had been walking on continued and seemed to disappear over the ridge to something interesting. I decided I would take a look a little farther up the dirt trail before turning around and making my way to the lush green ferns of the Fern Creek Trail.

I took a sip of water and started walking, and I suddenly found myself stepping in a muddy puddle of water—the same puddle I had encountered earlier. Barefoot and frozen, I was now disoriented and in disbelief—how was that possible? I was walking *up* the trail with the creek on the left side of me, and I would have had to physically turn one hundred and eighty degrees and start walking *down* the trail to be positioned where I was. But I never did turn around, so how did I get there? What happened to space and time? How could I have possibly arrived back there by going in the opposite direction? I turned around to see where I had been and then looked forward and down the track, noticing the creek was now on my right side. As I took notice of my position in space and stepped forward beyond the puddle of water, sounds of all kinds—rumblings, grumblings, twittering, chirping—flooded forcefully back into place. Not too much farther, I even heard human voices, and this time, I was glad to know they were part of the orchestral collective that filled the air.

The event in the redwood forest left an indelible mark inside me, but its enigmatic significance remained shrouded in the unimaginable until I was ready to imagine it and remember what I knew. I had to start by comprehending that as a human being, my natural ability to interact with the world is multidimensional,[11] that the true nature of human awareness is to perceive the multiple facets (or dimensions) of reality all at once, rather than being restricted and totally absorbed within a single one-dimensional aspect of reality at a time. That to perceive and feel the world that I cannot see, touch, smell, or hear, my belief system defining the properties of space and the qualities of time had to collide with and be inevitably overwhelmed by the experience of such multidimensionality, the fabric of existence itself.

Of course, we can all appreciate the defining role that space and time play in our everyday experience of life. We have long been intrigued by these two concepts, intuitively knowing that any reconceptualization of them and their relationship with each other can generate a whole new understanding of reality (which is what Einstein's theories did). Of the two, space seems the easier to experience—the physical walls defining a room, for example, provide us with a clear concept of the space of the room.

This notion of space, however, lacks depth; when our awareness is sharpened to conceive of and perceive the multidimensionality of space, this concept becomes highly pliable. In the forest, I had experienced it looping onto itself like a lemniscate, the curved glyph shaped like a figure eight on its side and used as a symbol of infinity in mathematics. The midpoint of this figure eight is, concurrently, the place of departure and arrival. To me, this is the point where I had found myself in the forest—a portal, where a myriad of separate spatial realities connect, becoming perceivable and traversable.[12]

It is because of this experience that my awareness was no longer absorbed in a one-dimensional spatial plane to the exclusion of all other possibilities. Finally, I started remembering what I knew—that I had had that experience before! A couple of years earlier, I had been standing in front of another portal. On that occasion, I was at Uluru in central Australia, visiting Uncle B in Mutitjulu. It was mid afternoon when I witnessed it open; that portal was not for me to cross but simply observe as it told its story and then closed right in front of my eyes. While I was able to perceive it, my awareness was unable to realize what was actually happening. It was only when I returned from the redwood forest that the knowing flooded in. I "remembered" how that portal had been used in the past to transfer "precious cargo"—the spirits of endangered sacred animals—from North America to Australia, in an effort to protect them till it was safe for them to return home. Elders of both countries keep this memory alive by telling the story of it, so we may not forget—we may not forget that it is all inscribed in the body of the Earth. Then I understood that, when I am ready to imagine it and remember it again, the Earth herself becomes my master storyteller. And the portal opens. Again.

So what about time? Oh, time is a whole other story—or two. Moving silently and unseen, time cannot be touched or tasted. Even though we don't really know what time is, we have always known it as immaterial and omnipresent; in more recent centuries, we have also come to believe it is something external to and independent of us, something "out there." Most recently, it announces itself through the beeping of smartphones that define the events in our lives, reinforcing this idea of time being outside.

And here I was confronted with my first point of collision—time is not out there; real time is, if anything, "in here." In fact, all organisms are innately endowed with an *internal* sense of time, a body clock regulating circadian rhythms. Humans, for example, come to grips with a world marked by recurrent time patterns, learning the length of time associated with the various events we've experienced every day since infancy. We are able to do so and keep track of time thanks to a small group of cells in our brain, which, together with a handful of genes, have the job to keep everything synchronized (and, by the way, these same time-keeping genes are found in all other animals, as well as in plants and microbes).

And even if we wander off into our individual offbeat tempos, our syncopated rhythms are consistently brought back to unison by the ultimate director of orchestra, the Earth, who perhaps synchronizes her whole system of biological metronomes through grand exhalations that burst out of her celestial skin into the cosmos.[13] Inevitably embedded in a world marked by recurrent time patterns as we are, it is by experiencing different lengths of time—the duration of events—and by paying attention to the event that is on offer at any given moment that we develop an awareness of time's presence and passing. This awareness truly is a gift; it makes the shared experience of life in this dimensional structure possible. By keeping us aligned with a coherent, linear flow of events, the feeling of past, present, and future delivers a deep sense of intimacy—a belonging within the unity of time and space, spirit and materiality, that all organisms living on the planet speak of through their gestures.

What the redwood forest in the Muir Woods had revealed was that the Earth's embrace grounds us all within this shared timescape, and it is precisely through this grounding that the gates to other dimensions of reality open. In other words, the awareness of this coherent background marks a steady reference position, the true point of departure to realize our capacity to move in and around the reference itself, time. And it is against this coherent backdrop that we can be alerted of the serendipitous occurrence of flawless incongruences, perfect glitches whose arrival allows for other dimensional potentialities to be perceived at all!

It seems, paradoxically, that our departure from and arrival to are exactly the same place; and as it had been the case for me with my puddle of muddy water in the forest, we may only understand our departure once we realize our arrival. I eventually comprehended that such capacity for unbound movement is our heritage as multidimensional beings. Correspondingly, by realizing the extent to which humanity is squandering such precious inheritance through a total misalignment from the only time that matters (in the literal sense of the earthly time that materializes this dimensional plane), the forest had informed my attention of the primary cause for the profound ecological crisis we are currently experiencing on the planet—the invention of time "out there."

Our modern notion of time as "out there" is a human invention, and its global normalization is a pretty recent phenomenon.[14] Of course, we have created devices to keep track of time and measure the various parts of a day for millennia—from tracking the movement of the sun with sundials and obelisks in ancient Egypt; the more advanced Greek clepsydrae, which measured time using the flow of water; and the Chinese candle clocks that relied on the rate of burning to mark the passing of time to the more recent invention of the hourglass, clock tower, pendulum, and mechanical alarm clock. While reflecting natural changes as the seasons or arbitrary changes as the week or the year, time had nevertheless remained a local (and solar) matter. It was the nineteenth-century globalizing world that succeeded at inventing and imposing a worldwide system of global time governance by supplanting local time; it turned time "out there" into a business that thrives on the collective preoccupation with ideologies of time saving, punctuality, and efficiency—the business of regulating and stabilizing the most precious of all commodities—our experience of life (time) itself.[15]

For sure, the invention of global time succeeded at simplifying operations within the railway systems, which allowed for their expansion, and more recently, supporting air traffic operations too. While mostly accepted with no objection, the decision to standardize time was, however, delivered with an exorbitant price tag, one that even someone with all the time in the world cannot (and should not) pay for. While promising to make many aspects of dealing with a globalized world easier, time "out there" had managed to abolish (for the most part) our multidimensional potentialities and possibilities by stealing time "in here." Regimented like a military action plan, the invention of time as "out there" did well at moving humanity to a false point of departure and increasingly dislocating us away from the connection to the Earth and the natural solar cycle, thereby inducing a loss of sight of the real eventual dimension of life itself.

This deceptive gimmick keeps us looping into a place of ordered uniformity, like the plants species we have enslaved in monoculture fields. While giving the illusion of revolutionary progress, the deception has devitalized us, like the plants we technologically manipulate, through our miserable and painful ignorance—ignorance of our true nature as human beings and of the true nature of the world around us.[16]

Time "out there" keeps us caught in a place of no power, a place from which we cannot arrive to our actual evolutionary destination as fully integrated, multidimensional beings. This is a highly dysfunctional state, a disease that should be treated as one. While the early signs are subtle and vague and may not be immediately obvious, this destructive condition worsens as it progresses and leads to premature death. At the individual level, the symptoms range from disorientation—we don't know who and where we are or where we are going—to poor or decreased judgment, so we become forgetful and confused, a danger to ourselves and others. It also leads from changes in personality—we become fearful, suspicious, apathetic, or uncommunicative—to loss of initiative, whereby we become passive and require prompting to become involved ... in anything. These are common symptoms of an individual suffering from a syndrome broadly defined as dementia. As humanity, we are suffering from a *collective* form of dementia.

Our symptomatic forgetfulness is robbing us of time "in here" by obliterating our capacity for re-membering ourselves and remembering who we are. In our state of utter confusion, we have come to believe it is acceptable to control the experience of time of all other forms of life, robbing them too of their right to existence. As the forest had warned, the invention of time "out there" is the primary cause for the profound ecological crisis the planet is currently experiencing. It is a form of violence, in which time is purely human and existence itself is reduced to an exclusively human affair.

This invention of time as human property that we own and control is probably one of the most sophisticated acts of planetary hegemony we have ever conceived, and, of course, it is a clear sign of the fundamental predicament—the deep delusion of separation—we have caught ourselves in. By replacing true time with an artificial, mechanical time that does not even exist, this device has succeeded in controlling humanity itself by abolishing (for the most part) its multidimensional potentialities and possibilities. If it is true that by controlling time you control everything, then reclaiming time "in here" is possibly the most powerful and revolutionary act of empowerment[17] we have to bring ourselves and the whole planet away from the brink into oblivion.

How do we get there? By absolute and pure ... chance! It is in chance, not control—variation, not homogeneity, and diversity, not uniformity—that existence thrives, evolves, develops, and learns. Chance is the untamed spirit of all-inclusive creativity, defiant of the safe rigidities imposed by control, which finds definition of itself by exclusion demarcating the boundaries of what is not. Chance is the dynamic continuity of existence that takes the exciting risk of inspiring the brilliance of this enchanted world. Chance is our antidote to the collective dementia we are entangled in—a medicinal nectar that flows to allow a different ending to our story.

That is what the redwood trees at Muir Woods had shown me through a point of collision, the paradox of my puddle of water. It is—was—collision, because the mind had to grapple with an experience that made no sense within the one-dimensional compartmentalization of the world (and any effort toward understanding it through logic still makes me go cross-eyed). But there it was, a muddy puddle of water in its intractable crystal clarity, which rendered the ruling point of denial pointless. So how did I get there? I was already there before arriving. By being so deeply grounded in the Earth's embrace, I found my true point of departure, from which the chance of moving in and around time and space became a possibility. And I was simply *there,* without understanding how I got there. The understanding did arrive, but much later.

It happened exactly two years later, thanks to the generous input of another conifer, the Monterey pine *(Pinus radiata),* a tinier cousin of the redwoods. From a forest plantation in South Australia, the pines had greeted me with an unwavering call—"flexibility is the key"—as they allowed the breeze to play with their needle-like hairs and sway their tall and slender bodies to and fro. A few weeks earlier, my research fellowship had come to an end, and so had my research position at the university.[18] For me, I had only just started making a meaningful contribution to science and society, and being pushed sideways and out was heartbreaking. Flexibility may very well be the key, but the truth was that as the pain of loss, grief, and anger circled around and around in my mind, I was struggling to find the gracefulness to trust and accept my new situation.

Lying there, on the ground, breathing in and out, the dark blue haze of the pines enveloped my body and colored me in. As I lay on the ground at their feet, the pines spoke softly: "Move not, but be moved—then everything is brought into being at the most perfect time." Then, loud and clear, I could feel the invisible but powerful pulse that nurtures and supports the dreaming of all life beating in my heart. I moved not, but let myself be moved. I didn't know that I was learning the steps of a new dance, the movement that would reconfigure my idea of time, space, and myself, the rhythm that would sing *this* book to me and through me. As I lay there on the ground, the trees continued, "All possibilities become available, and what truly needs to be done is done." And with that, a sense of great ease had come upon me.

Coda M

Your heart has eyes; look at the world with those eyes, and you will only see beauty.

~ The Very First Story ~

Memories—in the light, our memories are washed away, and we forget everything we knew. We forget who we are. It is in the darkness that we know the world. It is in the darkness that we know where we came from. The darkness remembers us, and when we remember who we are, we return to the most remarkable nothing.

It was the beginning of September in 2012. With its balmier weather and perfect blue-sky days, spring is a glorious time of the year in Western Australia. At this time, right at the heart of the wildflower season, a staggering twelve thousand species of plants—the largest collection of wildflowers in the world—burst into rich, multicolored blossoms, adorning the land with a finely woven tapestry like you will see nowhere else (quite literally, given that 60 percent of these plant species are endemic to this place and thus found only here). Emerging from a wintry hibernation, life turns into pulsating throbs and tingles, as when blood flow returns to your fingers after they have been exposed too long to the cold. And new beginnings are birthed.

"Do you remember the beginning? Your soft fingers rested, curled into tiny bunches as soon as they formed within the womb of the mother. And they stayed that way, neatly and securely tucked in, as you made your grand entrance into the light body of this world.[1] They are still curled into fists now, when you are sleeping and when you are not. Whether you realize it or not, you have kept them in that position ever since that beginning, as if holding onto something precious. Do you know why?" And so it spoke, the famous Peruvian duo better known as ayahuasca (*Banisteriopsis caapi,* the vine, and *Psychotria viridis,* also known as chacruna). In the perfect timing of new beginnings, they had come from afar to share with me a story of beginnings—actually, the very first story.

"Remember now. Since that beginning when you were a child-to-be, those two strong hands were curled firmly around the edges of an open map, *your* precious map. All the things you would experience, all that you had come to see and learn, was on it. While in the womb, with your eye still closed to this world, you had stared at your map over and over, considering all the adventures you would live (and sometimes you even kicked those excited little feet for the thrill that was to come). You were perfect and ready for it. Then, out of the infinite, you came into this world. Still holding your map open in front of your closed eyes, you were quick to sense how peculiar the light of this world was. Just like an overexposed photographic image, all the signposts, the descriptions of your life terrains, started fading out of your beautiful map, bleached by the light of this world, disappearing slowly as your earthly eyes opened. Soon, only fragments were left of what was meant to be the guiding map of your journey on Earth. But, child, your eyes only needed to adjust a little to see the entire map again, still open in front of you! Your seeing was replaced by an odd imagining, and you started believing in a story that was never yours." They spoke seamlessly, in a language of light, in which images are emanations of meanings arranged with beautiful exactness, and silent sounds are transmissions of truths that turn you from outside in, back to the pounding heart that rhythms you.

The image in my vision changed. The blue hues of the backdrop turned black, and the yellow tones I had seen became reds and browns. "They said this world is cruel. Since the beginning, you were told that this world is a place of struggle, a battlefield where you fight for survival. You were taught that your soft fingers and your gentle hands were for this fighting. Fighting to be right, fighting to be wrong, and if unsure, fighting anyhow. You learned this story very quickly. Again and again, you raised your hands, clenched into fists, to attack 'them,' defend yourself from 'them,' or even protect 'them' from themselves. It is a matter of survival, they said. This story, ah, you learned it so quickly. It took you a little longer to learn the truth of it. The truth is that you forgot *your* very first story in exchange for something not yours. Believing the story of those who had already forgotten theirs, you readily raised those fists without remembering why. Can you remember now?"

As the image changed again and the contours turned into greens and pinks, the vegetal ensemble continued. "Since the beginning of you, as that small child-to-be, your hands have rested in curled fists. Now, like then, you are not preparing for some fictional battle! Oh, no—you are holding your map tight, always open in front of eyes that you have closed to the reality of what you truly are. Now, just like ever, your hands are holding open the map that radiates through you a magical journey into this world. Your map has always been there; it's never been lost. Right now—as you have always done—you are holding it open with those hands of yours. But what you choose to see is up to you. Hands clenched into fists ready to judge and strike what has no meaning, would you really keep choosing, a play of smoking mirrors, the ghostly impressions the strange light of this world flickers in front of your eyes wide shut?

Or would you choose to open your eyes and see the portal—yes, the portal. Cross its threshold and open yourself to the path your map has always been showing you. This is the road of light leading forward to the beginning, a point of origin and arrival where all timelines and dreamscapes join. This—here, now—is the space where the separate parts dissolve and unify into the light that is the radiance of *you.* Ah, now you remember!"

And the Peruvian duo vanished, leaving behind the seed of a promise, the answer to the awkward *how* question: how do you open eyes that you think are open? At the time, I had not even a vague sense that in the darkness below the surface, the resolution to the riddle had already started germinating. But it had. And one spring, the promise bloomed.

It was the beginning of September in 2016 in Western Australia. Once again, life emerged from its wintry hibernation and turned into the pulsating rhythms that birth new beginnings. And so did I. After winter months of gestating the courage to venture into writing this book, the approaching spring had midwifed the delivery of the first chapter, and now it was persuading the little bud of the second chapter to unfurl its petals. This is when something unexpected happened, and the writing was halted for a couple of weeks (or so it seemed). A call had come, and I knew what to do.

Many years earlier, when I had visited Don M in Peru, he had told me that after a few *dietas* under the guidance of various *curanderos* (the plant shamans), the call comes to start dieting "unsupervised," alone with the plants. That time had come for me now, and the call was clear. I loaded my car with a few clothes, a box of green leafy vegetables and a bag of rice, some musical instruments, and my *mesa*—a portable altar, or "sacred medicine bundle," containing stones, herbs, and other personal artifacts used for healing, prayer, and ceremony.

I found myself driving south for five hours in the company of Picasso, my loyal canine assistant, to stay at the house of a friend who happened to be going away for a couple of weeks. We were headed toward the spectacular Rainbow Coast, where karri and tingle forests meet the Southern Ocean. There, the Valley of the Giants is home to some of the most ancient trees in the world, including the majestic four-hundred-year-old Giant Tingle Tree—the largest living eucalyptus known. The call had not come from the largest and oldest ones, though. Instead, the plant that had made the call was relatively small, short-lived, and not even native to the place. The plant that had made the call was one of the greatest spirits of all!

Open in the middle of the lounge, my *mesa* was decorated with fresh flowers I had collected during a short walk in the bushland surrounding my friend's place. I had arranged the flowers to encircle a small cup in the center of the *mesa.* Inside the cup, the dried leaves of the *mapacho*—also known by its common appellative, tobacco, or by its scientific name, *Nicotiana rustica*—had been soaking in water since the night before, making the cold-water extract almost ready for use. I drank it that night and began my one-on-one tuitions with this great teacher.

By the following afternoon, the spirit of the Tobacco approached me in animal form as I found myself lucid dreaming of a large anaconda appearing out of an immense ocean of water with its mouth wide open—there it was, the portal the Peruvian duo had described in the very first story several years before. Finally, the *how* question—how do you open your eyes to the reality that lies beyond the smoking mirrors and ghostly impressions of this world—was no longer awkward. The promised teaching was ready to blossom, and I knew its truth instinctively. In the same way, I knew that this was how Tobacco was inviting me to open my glorious map and cross the threshold into the beginning. As I did, he gifted me his precious *icaro de ayuda,* a medicine song to call for his assistance whenever it was required. For the nine days that followed, I walked between the worlds accompanied by this generous spirit, whose presence—I understand now—is a true gift to the world. He is the medicine that heals humanity's great grief.

"I have been with humanity for a long time," he said on the first day of the *dieta.* In a dream, Tobacco showed me the image of a bright jade-green tile emerging from pitch-black darkness. On the tile, a godlike character was depicted in a style that reminded me of an ancient Mayan glyph. And then I knew. Tobacco was revered for his sacredness and already used ceremonially back then, millennia before any European ever set foot in Mesoamerica.[2] "I am the Holy Spirit who connects you with Great Spirit, the God Creator, the Universal Mind, the Divine, or whatever name you want to use," he said. In that moment, I understood why this plant has been and still is so sacred to so many cultures, no matter the different geographical and historical backgrounds. "I am the one who heals humanity's grief, the deep sense of separation from God, that painful disconnection from the Universal Mind that makes you perceive yourself as alone and forsaken." He continued, "My child, humanity is drowning in an ocean of grief! You are filling up your lungs with this emotional pain to the point that you can no longer breathe. I meet these emotional waters with my holy fire and dry this disease out of your pure being. I bring peace."

Tobacco wasted no time, and within a couple of days from starting the *dieta,* I had clear visions of the plant in flower and what to use it for. He pointed out that his flowers are the best remedy for pulmonary conditions, specifically pneumonia.[3] At first, this information had seemed paradoxical to me—how could tobacco, a well-known cause of lung diseases, be the remedy for those conditions? My slight sense of disbelief did not faze him one bit. Quite the contrary, Tobacco carried on explaining why and when he turns into a poison. Then he proceeded to give precise instructions on when and how to prepare him into a medicine to heal pneumonia: "By affecting the proper functioning of the lungs and compromising the amount of oxygen that reaches the blood, pneumonia is, in fact, the physical manifestation of grief, the pain of separation in the emotional body."

At that point, something profound clicked in my mind, and Socoba's words—"the wisdom is in the oxygen, and the blood is the great connector"—echoed in my head. And there she was. Both Socoba and Tobacco were now present with me, but to my surprise, I could not tell them apart. They were both speaking—speaking as one. "At every breath, humanity opens its lungs. Within each breath, unifying molecules of oxygen infuse your humanity with their pure wisdom, the realization that you are not separate from the whole." Their perfect synchronicity produced a sense of deep calm, and the rhythmical flow of my breath was like a sacred hymn toned in unison with them.[4] "Without fear," they continued, "the blood brings this realization into the flow of embodiment, and in doing so, your truth—a state of communion with the whole—is made manifest via your heart."

And with that, Socoba vanished, as smoothly as she had appeared, leaving Tobacco to continue the conversation. "When constricted by grief, your lungs cannot open, the river of breath cannot flow, and the wisdom of oxygen cannot pour in. Prevented from realizing its very own nature, humanity is choking in this painful state and even getting somewhat accustomed—addicted—to it." He went on tenderly, "In each moment, humanity can open its eyes to close the rift that separates it from the whole by realizing that there is no rift at all. This realization heals the root cause of humanity's pain. Instead, it has looked for a quick relief from its effects, filling up the lungs with my smoke to bring a temporary peace away from a pain it forgot it never needed. Instead of asking for complete healing, humanity has misused me as a partial sedative—this abuse turned me into a poison."

At this point, Tobacco paused. He was giving me the space to listen to a question I didn't know I had asked: how do we actually heal this grief through realization? In answer to it, he offered up an image. A golden map materialized in my vision, accompanied by the feeling of something I had seen before, the sense of knowing, a memory. Then I heard, "My child, you are grieving for the loss of something you never lost. You *believe* you lost your precious map, the one guiding your magical journey into this world and always reminding you the truth of who you are. But see, that map is open in front of you right now."

All of a sudden, I knew Tobacco was no longer alone. Joined by the Ayahuasca Vine and Chacruna, they spoke together as one, "Your seeing was replaced by a story that was never yours, but you believed it to be! You have come to define who you are by this insane belief. It is certain, then, that all of your perceptions would be insane. It is predictable that you would perceive your very existence coming under threat when the belief of what you are is under attack. As the imaginary victim of a hypothetical aggressor, the 'identity' given to you by your belief sees the threat of its possible annihilation, and in self-defense, it calls for attack. At its command, you fight; you raise your fists not really knowing why. Or do you?"

With a soothing tone, they continued, "Child, of course you feel disoriented and scared! You believe in what do not exist. You believe in who you are *not*. But know this. You, that glorious beam of light that traveled across the infinite to be born into the body of this world, always were; you existed before any belief system, before anything and after everything. How can you truly lose your map? How can you truly forget your very first story? Grief and the pain exist only in your belief! You *are* your glorious map; you *are* your very first story. You are the *only* story there is." As the Ayahuasca Vine and Chacruna disappeared with a triumphant smile, a luminous imprint started glowing in the field of my vision. "Forgiveness," whispered Tobacco, "this alone illuminates the way out of the maze humanity has created with all its beliefs."

Once again, Tobacco answered my question before I knew I had asked it. "Forgiveness is not a *doing.* It is an *undoing* of the imaginary 'self,' the one you have come to believe you are. The arrival of forgiveness calls for the annihilation of this counterfeiter and its belief system. Be vigilant! This mock *doing* of yourself will strike its final deceptive manoeuver to keep you trapped in its maze in a state of separation—the belief that you do not deserve forgiveness because you are guilty of all possible wrongdoings. But this is simply not the truth, because you are none of your doings. Accept this, even if you do not understand this now. Accept this, and you will remember who you are. Accept this, and you will *know* it to be true. And through this, you will realize that, in the end, the love that you are does not need forgiveness at all!"

A flooding of tears washed over me, inside and out. I finally understood. Inside the maze of smoking mirrors, ghostly impressions, and bleak illusions with no meaning, we never feel safe and at home. Believing that we lack everything, we keep *doing* by seeking something that we need without even knowing what that something actually is. What we truly are does not lack anything, does not seek or need anything, because it is already *being* everything. Tobacco was right; forgiveness is not a doing, but an emerging out of all illusions, a waking that dissolves the grief of separation and simultaneously returns us to ourselves, to the only reality we cannot not be—to love. Here, we find peace. Here, I found peace.

***

"Here is the very first and the very last story of you. Stories are a learning tool for the soul. Once you remember who we are, you no longer need any story at all." Thus spoke the plant.

ENDNOTES

Prelude

[1]   A longer version of this story can be found here: M. Gagliano, "In the Eye of the Beholder: A Personal Story of Two Seeds," Sydney Environmental Institute, University of Sydney, May 10, 2017, http://sydney.edu.au/environme nt-institute/blog/in-the-eye-of-the-beholder-a-pe rsonal-story-of-two-seeds.

Chapter O

[1]   Plants don't have a skin as such, but they do have dermal tissue, or epidermis, to protect their inner from the outer.

[2]   When the leaves of *Himatanthus sucuuba* are broken off their stems, and when the stems are broken from the branches, a milky-white fluid material, latex, is exuded. Wounding the tree bark will also exude the latex. The latex of this tree is a popular natural remedy in Peruvian herbalism, and its long-standing use for healing wounds was verified by Peruvian researchers in an animal study published in 1997 (see L. Villegas, I.D. Fernández, H. Maldonado, R. Torres, A. Zavaleta, A.J. Vaisberg, and G.B. Hammond, "Evaluation of the Wound-Healing

Activity of Selected Traditional Medicinal Plants from Peru." *Journal of Ethnopharmacology* 55 (1997): 193–200). *Himatanthus sucuuba* is one of more than twenty thousand plant species from forty different families that produce latex. Despite its ubiquity, which attests to its biological significance, the function of latex in nature is not fully understood. It is most likely used by the plants as part of a defensive mechanism against herbivory such as the delivery of anti-herbivory compounds and rapid wound healing. See G. Bauer, C. Friedrich, C. Gillig, F. Vollrath, T. Speck, and C. Holland, "Investigating the Rheological Properties of Native Plant Latex," *Journal of the Royal Society Interface* 11 (2014): 20130847.

[3]   *Mapacho* is a potent variety of natural jungle tobacco. Its smoke is considered of utmost importance for its role as the mediator between the shaman and all other plant spirits. For details on the preparation of the various forms of tobacco and their uses (ritual, medical, and otherwise) in South America, as well as an extensive bibliographic reference list to earlier works, see Johannes Wilbert, *Tobacco and Shamanism in South America* (New Haven, CT: Yale University Press, 1987).

[4]   It is during such a process that the student learns how to connect with the spirit of that particular plant, which will instruct him or her

through visions and songs. In the Western world, this kind of shamanic work is often equated with the use of the psychoactive herbal brew known as *ayahuasca.* And indeed, the ayahuasca movement in the West has gained incredible popularity over the last few decades. Yet all *vegetalistas* (plant shamans) are adamant about the crucial importance of the *dieta* and insist on the fact that the real work of becoming familiar and sensitive to the spirit of the plants and their teachings takes place during the isolating period of the *dieta.* Because of this, attending ayahuasca ceremonies alone will not take the student far. For an overview of the topic, see Luis Eduardo Luna, *Vegetalismo: Shamanism Among the Mestizo Population of the Peruvian Amazon* (Stockholm: Almqvist & Wiksell International, 1986). See also, L.E. Luna, "The Healing Practices of a Peruvian Shaman," *Journal of Ethnopharmacology* 11 (1984): 123–133; and L.E. Luna, "The Concept of Plants As Teachers Among Four Mestizo Shamans of Iquitos, Northeastern Perú," *Journal of Ethnopharmacology* 11 (1984): 135–156. For specific details on the *dieta,* see chapter 5 in Stephan Beyer, *Singing to the Plants: A Guide to Mestizo Shamanism in the Upper Amazon* (Albuquerque: University of New Mexico Press, 2009), 52–62).

[5] See, for example, N. Fakhrudin, B. Waltenberger, M. Cabaravdic, A.G. Atanasov, C. Malainer, D. Schachner, E.H. Heiss et al. "Identification of Plumericin As a Potent New Inhibitor of the NF-kB Pathway with Anti-Inflammatory Activity in Vitro and in Vivo," *British Journal of Pharmacology* 171, no.7 (2014): 1676–1686.

[6] From the modern (Western) scientific perspective, knowledge regarding the medicinal properties of plants was developed by our ancestors through millennia of hands-on experience gained by trial and error. According to this story, this body of knowledge was then transmitted orally, passed down from one generation to the next as part of our cultural traditions. For a discussion on the epistemological problem of this view, see Stephen Harrod Buhner, *The Lost Language of Plants: The Ecological Importance of Plant Medicines for Life on Earth* (White River Junction, VT: Chelsea Green, 2002), 43–47. See also David Abram, *The Spell of the Sensuous:Perception and Language in a More-Than-Human World* (New York: Vintage Books, 1997), 115–117.

[7] See discussion of Plato's *Phaedrus* in Michael Marder, *The Philosopher's Plant: An Intellectual Herbarium* (New York: Columbia University Press, 2014), 3–18.

[8]   See Pam Montgomery, *Plant Spirit Healing: A Guide to Working with Plant Consciousness* (Rochester, VT: Bear, 2008), 98.

[9]   See Montgomery, *Plant Spirit Healing,* 180.

[10]   Thanks to the four iron atoms of the pigment heme, the component that gives blood its red color, hemoglobin is able to mingle with the oxygen available in the lungs and then load and transport those precious atoms into the tissues of the body. Once the oxygen is released, globin, the protein component of hemoglobin, is able to combine with carbon dioxide and carry it back to the lungs where it can be realized. A less widely known fact, however, is that hemoglobins have been known to exist in plants, and, most intriguingly, these proteins may have a common function and similar history of evolutionary adaptations in both plants and animals. For reviews on the topic, see, for example, V. Garrocho-Villegas, S.K. Gopalasubramaniam, and R. Arredondo-Peter, "Plant Hemoglobins: What We Know Six Decades After Their Discovery," *Gene* 398 (2007): 78–85; and S. Kuntu, J.T. Trent, and M.S. Hargrove, "Plants, Humans and Hemoglobins." *Trends in Plant Science* 8, no.8 (2003): 387–393.

[11]   In the Western metaphysical tradition, for example, Aristotle philosophized over the

existence of the soul—from the ancient Greek ψυχή (*psuche,* "breath of life")—as that which makes an organism an organism at all, and the idea of a vegetative or nutritive soul that epitomizes plants but is also present within all animals, including human beings. See Aristotle's nested hierarchy of soul functions in books 2 and 3 of *De Anima (On the Soul)* (London: Penguin Classics, 1987).

[12]   Echoing the famous Heraclitus fragment 123, "loves to hide," referring to the cryptic and elusive nature of plant life. See Michael Marder, *Plant-Thinking: A Philosophy of Vegetal Life* (New York: Columbia University Press, 2013, 28).

[13]   See Marder, *The Philosopher's Plant,* 13.

[14]   For a definition and brief history of empathy, see E. Clarke, T. DeNora, and J. Vuoskoski, "Music, Empathy, and Cultural Understanding," *Physics of Life Reviews* 15 (2015): 61–88. For an in-depth discussion on empathy and plants, see M. Marder, "The Life of Plants and the Limits of Empathy," *Dialogue* 51, no.2 (2012): 259–273.

[15]   In the words of philosopher Edmund Husserl, this experience of the other is a kind of "original reciprocal co-existence." See discussion of the topic in D. Zahavi, "Husserl's Intersubjective Transformation of Transcendental

Philosophy," *Journal of the British Society for Phenomenology* 27, no.7 (1996): 228–245. See also Dan Zahavi, *Self and Other: Exploring Subjectivity, Empathy, and Shame* (Oxford: Oxford University Press, 2015).

[16]   For an introductory overview on ayahuasca, see Stephan Beyer, *Singing to the Plants,* 207–212.

[17]   Each *icaro* is a direct line of communication between the plant and the human. Because of its multidimensional nature, it is difficult to distinguish between singing and listening while one sings it; it seems more accurate to say that *icaros* are constantly singing themselves. A useful overview about what *icaros* are and how they are used can be found in Stephan Beyer, *Singing to the Plants,* 63–80.

[18]   See David Abram's discussion of Merleau-Ponty in *The Spell of the Sensuous,* 66–67.

[19]   M. Gagliano, M. Renton, N. Duvdevani, M. Timmins, and S. Mancuso, "Out of Sight but Not Out of Mind: Alternative Means of Communication in Plants." *PLoS ONE* 7, no.5 (2012): e37382. See also M. Gagliano, M. Renton, N. Duvdevani, M. Timmins, and S. Mancuso, "Acoustic and Magnetic Communication in Plants: Is It Possible? Plant Signaling & Behavior 7, no.10 (2012): 1346–1348.

Chapter R

[1] Generally, the term *philanthropist* is used to indicate a wealthy human who assists charitable causes by giving money and time. Here the term is applied to plants in the original meaning of the word—derived from the Latin *philanthropia,* which, in turn, was derived from the ancient Greek *philanthropos* ("loving humanity" from *phil-,* "loving" and *anthropos,* "humanity")—by referring to the sense of caring, nourishing, supporting, and enhancing the human being.

[2] Matthew Hall offers an in-depth discussion of environmental ethics and indigenous worldviews in his book *Plants As Persons: A Philosophical Botany* (Albany: State University of New York Press, 2011), 99–117.

[3] See M. Gagliano, M. Renton, N. Duvdevani, M. Timmins, and S. Mancuso, "Out of Sight but Not Out of Mind: Alternative Means of Communication in Plants." *PLoS ONE* 7, no.5 (2012): e37382.

[4] "The history of science teaches that the greatest advances in the scientific domain have been achieved by bold thinkers who perceived new and fruitful approaches that others failed to notice."—Louis de Broglie, Nobel laureate, April 25, 1978.

[5]   See Thomas Kuhn's revolutionary and controversial book *The Structure of Scientific Revolutions* (Chicago: University of Chicago Press, 1962). A fiftieth anniversary edition of this work was published in 2012.

[6]   For a recent overview, see Richard Karban, "The Language of Plant Communication (and How It Compares to Animal Communication," in *The Language of Plants: Science, Philosophy, Literature,* ed. M. Gagliano, John C. Ryan, and Patrícia Vieira, 3–26 (Minneapolis: University of Minnesota Press, 2017); and Robert Raguso and André Kessler, "Speaking in Chemical Tongues: Decoding the Language of Plant Volatiles," also in Gagliano, Ryan, and Vieira, *Language of Plants,* 27–61.

[7]   In his stimulating personal perspective on elements of the scientific method and the attributes of a scientist searching for the truth, Irvin Rothchild, an emeritus professor of reproductive biology, has asked, "Shouldn't a scientific paper be at least as much fun to read as a good detective story?" See I. Rothchild, "Induction, Deduction, and the Scientific Method: An Eclectic Overview of the Practice of Science" (Madison, WI: Society for the Study of Reproduction, 2006), 1–13.

[8]   See H.R. Maturana, "Science and Daily Life: The Ontology of Scientific Explanations," in

Self-organization: Portrait of a Scientific Revolution, ed. W. Krohn, G. Küppers, and H. Nowotny, 12–35, Sociology of the Sciences Yearbook 14. (Dordrecht, Netherlands: Springer, 1990).

[9]   The term *three sisters* refers to corn, beans, and squash plants. The three sisters system is the famous traditional Native American method of growing these plants together as companions, as well as eating them together—as they complement each other nutritionally—and celebrating them together as precious life-giving gifts from the Great Spirit (according to Iroquois legend). Today, corn is one of the most genetically modified plant species. It is kind of ironic, then, that the same plant that is so heavily subjected to biotechnological manipulations, including RNA silencing, was also the first plant to "speak up."

[10]   The French poet Francis Ponge said, "they have no voice" (ils n'ont pas de voix). Ponge's statement seems to be confirmed by our experience of a walk in nature, and yet it is so far from the truth. See M. Marder and M. Gagliano, 2013, "How Do Plants Sound?" Columbia University Press Blog, www.cupblog. org/?p=10609, and also republished in Marder's book *Grafts* (Minneapolis, MN: Univocal, 2016), 101–102.

[11]   See discussion on the term *voice* in E.K. Watts, "'Voice' and 'Voicelessness' in Rhetorical Studies," *Quarterly Journal of Speech* 87, no.2 (2001): 179–196.

[12]   See discussion in Jennifer Peeples and Stephen Depoe, eds., *Voice and Environmental Communication* (Basingstoke, U.K.: Palgrave Macmillan, 2014) specifically, chap.9, "The Language That All Things Speak: Thoreau and the Voice of Nature," by William Homestead, 183–204. See also E.K. Watts, "'Voice' and 'Voicelessness' in Rhetorical Studies," *Quarterly Journal of Speech* 87, no.2 (2001): 179–196.

[13]   As argued by S. Vogel, "The Silence of Nature," *Environmental Values* 15, no.2 (2006): 145–171.

[14]   See M. Gagliano, "Green Symphonies: A Call for Studies on Acoustic Communication in Plants," *Behavioral Ecology* 24, no.4 (2012): 789–796.

[15]   See M. Gagliano, S. Mancuso, and D. Robert, "Towards Understanding Plant Bioacoustics," *Trends in Plant Science* 17, no.6 (2012): 323–25.

[16]   This applies to members of human communities as well as nonhuman others.

[17]   For an in-depth discussion on the topic, see M. Gagliano, John C. Ryan, and Patrícia Vieira,

eds., *The Language of Plants: Science, Philosophy, Literature* (Minneapolis: University of Minnesota Press, 2017), and specifically chap.5, "To Hear Plants Speak," by Michael Marder, 103–125 and chap.14, "In the Key of Green? The Silent Voices of Plants in Poetry," by John C. Ryan, 273–296.

[18] Devices, which assign a "musical" voice to plants and make them "sing," have been around since the seventies. These are nothing more than multimeters that measure electric current, voltage, resistance in DC current, and impedance in AC circuits; they have been modified so that they detect the impedance from a leaf to the root system and then use a MIDI interface to arbitrarily assign musical notes to different ranges of voltage values. These gadgets have become increasingly popular and may be quite appealing at first, as they appear to create a tangible connection between the human and the plant by claiming to offer a direct experience of a plant "voice" (and in the same case, stretching it further to plant intelligence and consciousness). Sadly, the sounds emitted by these devices are not the sounds emitted by the plant. Instead, they merely are the electrical signals filtered through set notes that produce the experience of "plant music." Scientifically speaking, there is a significant difference between the acoustic and

vibrational signals of a plant and its electrical circuitry, as the two signals are of different natures. But aside from this, there is another simple reason why such an approach to plants has no integrity. Just consider this: humans also produce electricity and can be plugged in to these devices and made to "sing." However, nobody would believe that the sound coming from such a device is, in fact, the voice of the human. However, in the case of plants, we are misled into believing that the sound coming from the device is, in fact, a plant's voice. Like the human, plants have their own voice, and there is no need to use their electrical signals to produce a surrogate voice. While such devices may have had their place in the seventies, their immature anthropocentric approach is disrespectful, as it overrides the agency of the other (the plant) and, as such, reveals the same abusive mind-set responsible for the disregard and the destruction of plants and nature. The "music of plants" may be portrayed as a scientific exploration into the communicative world of plants and may seem to carry the promise of deepening our understanding of plant perception and intelligence, but our ignorance is dangerous. For those who care not to ignore but look beyond the surface, you will soon realize that this approach to plants is far from enlightening.

Chapter Y

[1]   For example, see Michael Harner, *The Way of the Shaman* (New York: HarperOne, 1990); Hank Wesselman, *The Spiritwalker: Messages from the Future* (New York: Bantam, 1996); and Hank Wesselman, *The Journey to the Sacred Garden: A Guide to Traveling in the Spiritual Realms* (Carlsbad, CA: Hay House, 2012.

[2]   A member of the parsley family, osha *(Ligusticum porteri)* is an important ethnobotanical plant with a pungent and distinctively spicy root. It has long been used for both ceremonial and medicinal purposes by various Native American tribes, including the Apache, Navaho, Ute, Zuni, and Lakota. The plant is known as "bear root" because it is thought that Native Americans learned of its use by observing bears digging up roots to eat or rub in their fur, possibly to repel insects and soothe bites, a behavior known as "self-medication." Indeed, not only bears but also chimpanzees, starlings, grackles, caterpillars, and ants are known to use medicinal plants to prevent and treat ailments, making self-medication a practice humans share with other animal species. For examples, see D.H. Clayton and N.D. Wolfe, "The Adaptive Significance of Self-Medication," *Trends in Ecology and Evolution* 8, no.2 (1993): 60–63;

M.A. Huffman "Self-Medicative Behavior in the African Great Apes: An Evolutionary Perspective into the Origins of Human Traditional Medicine," *BioScience* 51, no.8 (2001): 651–661; M.A. Huffman, "Animal Self-Medication and Ethno-Medicine: Exploration and Exploitation of the Medicinal Properties of Plants," *Proceedings of the Nutritional Society* 62 (2003): 371–381; P. Christe, A. Oppliger, F. Bancalà, G. Castella, and M. Chapuisat, "Evidence for Collective Medication in Ants," *Ecology Letters* 6 (2003): 19–22; E.M. Costa-Neto, "Zoopharmacognosy: The Self-Medication Behavior of Animals," *Interfaces Científicas—Saúde e Ambiente* 1, no.1 (2012): 61–72; M.S. Singer, K.C. Mace, and E.. Bernays, "Self-Medication As Adaptive Plasticity: Increased Ingestion of Plant Toxins by Parasitized Caterpillars," *PLoS ONE* 4, no.3 (2009): e4796.

Chapter N

[1]   In *Elements of the Science of Botany, As Established by Linnaeus; with Examples to Illustrate the Classes and Orders of his System* (London: T. Bensley for J. Murray, 1812), Richard Duppa reported that the plant was already known by both Theophrastus (c.371–287BCE), the ancient Greek philosopher and favorite pupil of Aristotle, and by Pliny the Elder (c.23–79 CE), the ancient Roman naturalist. However, the first formal description

of the plant was by Carl Linnaeus in his *Species Plantarum* (Laurentius Salvius, 1753). From the sixteenth to the eighteenth century, *Mimosa* figured prominently in the work of many naturalists and botanists, who were intrigued by the seismonastic movements of the plant (the closing of the leaves in response to touch) as well as its nyctinastic movements (the drooping of the leaves in response to the onset of darkness—sometimes still referred to as "sleeping movements"). See, for example, John Hill, *The Sleep of Plants and Cause of Motion in the Sensitive Plant, Explain'd.* (London, 1757); and Charles Darwin, *The Power of Movement in Plants* (London, 1880). *Mimosa* also inspired several poets and became a popular subject of literature, including in Erasmus Darwin's *The Botanic Garden* (J. Johnson, 1781). As pointed out by Sam George, "It became a symbol of human sensibility in Cowper's 'The Poet, The Oyster and the Sensitive Plant' (1782) and was used to explore sentiency in nature and human feeling in Shelley's 'The Sensitive Plant' (1820). The sensitive plant was also a metaphor for male and female genitalia in bawdy works: James Perry's 'Mimosa' (1779) contains phallic imagery." See S. George "Carl Linnaeus, Erasmus Darwin and Anna Seward: Botanical Poetry and Female Education," *Science and Education* 23 (2014): 673–694.

[2] Garcia de Orta, *Colóquios dos simples e drogas he cousas mediçinais da India* (Goa, 1563); Castor Durante da Gualdo, *Herbario Nuovo* (Venice, 1636).

[3] Johann David Mauchart, *De herba mimosa seu sentiente* (Tübingen, 1688); Étienne Chauvin, *Lexicon rationale sive thesaurus philosophicum ordine alphabetico digestus* (Rotterdam, 1692).

[4] Giacomo Zanoni, *Istoria botanica* (Bologna, 1675).

[5] Juliet, speaking to Romeo: "What's in a name? That which we call a rose/By any other name would smell as sweet." William Shakespeare, *Romeo and Juliet,* 2.2.43–44, http://shakespear e.mit.edu/romeo_juliet.

[6] See R.M. Maniquis, "The Puzzling 'Mimosa': Sensitivity and Plant Symbols in Romanticism," *Studies in Romanticism* 8, no.3 (1969): 129–155. See also www.nybg.org/poetic-botany/mimosa, the New York Botanical Garden's beautiful digital exhibition titled *Poetic Botany: Art and Science of the Eighteenth-Century Vegetable World,* which brings together many of the historical as well as contemporary resources on this plant (and others). And Ivan Henriques's artwork at www.i vanhenriques.com/works/jurema-action-plant, where *Mimosa pudica* features as the "action plant" in an interactive bio-machine.

[7]   The Aristotelian perspective on the sensorial world continues having a profound and long-lasting influence on modern thought. For a recent review of the topic, see, for example, A.P. Bos, "Aristotle on the Difference Between Plants, Animals, and Human Beings and on the Elements As Instruments of the Soul (*De Anima* 2.4.415b18)," The Review of Metaphysics 63, no.4 (2010): 821–841. Philosophical reflections aside, this is a core theme I will discuss recurrently throughout this book because of its huge repercussions on the modus operandi of modern society and, most importantly, on the current state of the environment at a planetary scale.

[8]   Although scholars are yet to agree conclusively on its origins, the commedia dell'arte was an early form of professional theater that began in Italy in the early sixteenth century and quickly spread across Europe. It is characterized by the use of masks, improvisation, and its famous character types: the servants, the old men, the lovers, and the captains. See Winifred Smith, *The Commedia dell'Arte: A Study in Italian Popular Comedy* (New York: Columbia University Press, 1912). For some examples of recent scholarship on the topic, see Robert Henke's *Performance and Literature in the Commedia dell'Arte* (Cambridge: Cambridge University Press, 2002); M.A. Katritzky, "The Commedia dell'Arte:

New Perspectives and New Documents," *Early Theatre* 11, no.2, 1 (2008): 141–154; R. Henke, "Back to the Future: A Review of Comparative Studies in Shakespeare and the Commedia dell'Arte," *Early Theatre* 11, no.2, 1 (2008): 227–240. Further resources on the history of the commedia dell'arte are also available here: www.commedia-dell-arte.com.

[9] See Joseph Campbell, *The Hero with a Thousand Faces* (New World Library, 2008), a seminal work in which Campbell outlines the structure of any mythical journey in all its phases and archetypal motifs.

[10] Just like in T.S. Eliot's poem "Little Gidding," the last poem of *Four Quartets* (1942). The main theme of the poem is time and eternity, and "Little Gidding" exemplifies the cyclic progression of human understanding. See T.S. Eliot, *Four Quartets* (New York: Faber & Faber, 2001); also M. Gagliano, "Persons As Plants: Ecopsychology and the Return to the Dream of Nature," *Landscapes: The Journal of the International Centre for Landscape and Language* 5, no.2 (2013), http://ro.ecu.edu.au /landscapes/vol5/iss2/14.

[11] M. Gagliano, M. Renton, M. Depczynski, and S. Mancuso, "Experience Teaches Plants to Learn Faster and Forget Slower in Environments

Where It Matters," *Oecologia* 175 (2014): 63–72.

[12]   The overall reaction to the "*Mimosa* experiment" as well as the not-so-well founded scientific criticisms and the explicit intellectual intolerance and even vulgarity were masterfully captured by Michael Pollan in his "The Intelligent Plant," an essay based on events that took place at the scientific meeting on plant signaling and behavior held in Vancouver earlier that year. See Michael Pollan, "The Intelligent Plant" *The New Yorker,* December 23, 2013; see also M. Gagliano, C.A. Abramson, and M. Depczynski, "Plants Learn and Remember: Let's Get Used to It," *Oecologia* 186 (2018): 29–31.

[13]   The American evolutionary biologist Ernst Mayr defined the nature of causation in biology over fifty years ago. He made the distinction between *proximate* causes as the immediate, mechanical influences on a specific trait and *ultimate* causes as those explaining the historical evolution of an organism. The proximate–ultimate dyad has shaped the perspective of most contemporary biologists, as well as philosophers of science, and it is still widely accepted today. See Ernst Mayr, "Cause and Effect in Biology," *Science* 134, no.3489 (1961): 1501–1506; and for an alternative perspective on the topic, K.N. Laland, K. Sterelny, J. Odling-Smee, W. Hoppitt,

and T. Uller, "Cause and Effect in Biology Revisited: Is Mayr's Proximate-Ultimate Dichotomy Still Useful?" *Science* 334, no.6062 (2011): 1512–1516. For further discussion of this topic, see also M. Gagliano, J.C. Ryan, and P. Vieira, introduction to *The Language of Plants: Science, Philosophy, Literature,* vii–xxxiii (Minneapolis: University of Minnesota Press, 2017).

[14] Generally, we are accustomed to seeing the term *flesh* in reference to the soft muscular and fatty tissue that covers the bones of vertebrate animals and using *meat* to describe the animal flesh we consume as food. The term *flesh* is equally appropriate for plant tissues, especially pulpy and juicy plant parts like fruits and vegetables. Although edible and consumed as food, we don't refer to plant flesh as *meat.* I am aware of only one exception where the flesh of a plant is called *meat* when consumed. This is the case for the *hikuri,* the peyote cactus *(Lophophora williamsii)* used by the Wixarika people of the Sierra Madre Occidental in Mexico and by the Native American Church in United States in their traditional shamanic practices.

[15] See Michael Marder, *Plant-Thinking: A Philosophy of Vegetal Life* (New York: Columbia University Press, 2013), 179–188); A. Pelizzon and M. Gagliano, "The Sentience of Plants:

194

Animal Rights and Rights of Nature Intersecting?" *Australian Animal Protection Law Journal* 1 (2015): 5–13.

[16] Earlier investigations of *Mimosa* had studied the plant's behavior by literally cutting its leaves and experimenting on them in Petri dishes. For example, Philip Applewhite describes such an experiment as, "From each plant, leaves ... were excised and floated in water, a standard procedure ... that does not damage the leaves, in a plastic petri dish." Similarly, Fondeville and colleagues describe the standard procedure: "The intermediately developed pinnae were cut from the plants and floated on water under fluorescent illumination.... They were tested at intervals for sensitivity to touch." For details, see P.B. Applewhite, "Behavioral Plasticity in the Sensitive Plant, *Mimosa*," Behavioural Biology 7 (1972): 47–53; and J.C. Fondeville, H.A. Borthwick, and S.B. Hendricks, "Leaflet Movement of *Mimosa pudica* Indicative of Phytochrome Action," *Planta* 69 (1966): 357–364.

[17] For an accessible and remarkable exploration of this issue, see Terence McKenna, *Food of the Gods: The Search for the Original Tree of Knowledge: A Radical History of Plants, Drugs and Human Evolution* (London: Rider Books, 1999).

[18]   See M. Gagliano, 2015. "In a Green Frame of Mind: Perspectives on the Behavioral Ecology and Cognitive Nature of Plants," *AoB Plants* 7 (2015): plu075; also refer to Nancy E. Baker, "The Difficulty of Language: Wittgenstein on Animals and Humans, in *Language, Ethics and Animal Life,* ed. N. Forsberg, M. Burley, and N. Hämäläinen, 45–64 (New York: Bloomsbury, 2002).

[19]   The literal meaning of the word *anthropocentric* refers to placing the human in the center of the universal stage. Interestingly, its application is not even coherent with its own meaning, which somehow highlights the intrinsic madness of it. In fact, as if the human being as the reference point in the "center" was not enough, we have fabricated a new point and moved ourselves there, at the "top." This positioning constrains all other species to a "below" position and simultaneously forces our idea of the universal stage itself to conform to a pyramidal shape.

[20]   Implicit bias, automatic stereotypes, and prejudice had long been assumed to be fixed behavioral responses, the influence of which was inescapable as it occurred without conscious control. However, we now know that these attitudes are malleable and responsive to a wide range of strategic, social, and contextual influences. For some examples, see

I. Blair, "The Malleability of Automatic Stereotypes and Prejudice," *Personality and Social Psychology Review* 6, no.3 (2002): 242–261; and L. Roos, S. Lebrecht, J.W. Tanaka, and M.J. Tarr, "Can Singular Examples Change Implicit Attitudes in the Real-World?" *Frontiers in Psychology* 4 (2013): 594. Further, the topic in this specific context was discussed in the Gagliano et al., introduction to *The Language of Plants.*

Chapter G

[1]   Don J was a victim of *brujeria* (witchcraft) and passed away in 2016.

[2]   This plant is known to be resistant to a high degree of aridity; while dieting with it, Piñon blanco showed me that he bestows the same capacity to endure strenuous conditions on humans by increasing their stamina and supporting their immune system.

[3]   In my dream, the spirit of this plant had presented himself a medical doctor, though I was totally unaware at the time that the plant had the genus name *Jatropha,* which is derived from the Greek words *iatrós* (doctor) and *trophé* (food), which implies the traditional medicinal role of this plant across countries. See D.M.R. Prasad, A. Izam, and M.R. Khan, "*Jatropha curcas:* Plant of Medical Benefits," *Journal of*

Medicinal Plants Research 6, no.14 (2012): 2691–2699.

[4]   Ayahuma refers here to *Couroupita guianensis*, a tree native to the tropical forests of northeastern South America. However, Ayahuma is also the name of one of the main protagonists of the Inti Raymi—the Inca Festival of the Sun, which takes place annually toward the end of June in the Andean villages of Peru, Bolivia, Argentina, and Ecuador. The festival is an occasion for celebrating the life-giving power of the sun, as well as giving thanks for the harvest, hence a perfect time for renewing and strengthening the relationship with Pachamama—Mother Earth. As part of the celebrations, the Ayahuma leads a ritual performance in which a group of dancers go around in circles (representing the equinoxes and solstices) while stamping their feet to encourage Mother Earth to be rejuvenated for the new agricultural cycle. The Ayahuma wears a brightly colored hand-knitted mask, which has become an icon of the Andean folklore. A link between the symbolic and the real (interior-exterior), his two-faced mask represents the duality of the world: past and future, day and night, good and bad. The mask also bears twelve horns (representing the twelve months of the year) and other attachments that look like antennas (representing snakes, an Andean

symbol of wisdom). When the Spaniards first encountered it during the colonization of South America, they considered the Ayahuma and his mask as the depiction of a demonic character. However, for the indigenous people, the Ayahuma is the materialization of the energies of Pachamama (i.e., the vital life forces found in nature) and hence is highly respected.

[5]   Ivan Pavlov was a Russian physiologist who discovered a new type of learning—associative learning—whereby his dogs learned to associate the sound of a bell to the arrival of food. For a description of Pavlov's experiment see: S.A. McLeod, "Pavlov's Dogs," Simply Psychology, 2013, www.simplypsychology.org/pavlov.html.

[6]   The tree has been known in India for at least three thousand years. According to some scholars, European traders brought it to the subcontinent; others propose a more ancient migration route. See J.L. Sorenson and C.L. Johannessen, "Scientific Evidence for Pre-Columbian Transoceanic Voyages," *Sino-Platonic Papers* 133 (2004).

[7]   According to Hindu tradition, the cannonball tree is sacred because the flower petals resemble the hood of the "Naga," a sacred snake protecting the stigma known as the "Shiva lingham"; it symbolizes the sanctified phallus and the serpent protector of elemental sexual energy. The tree's

other names, "nagalinga" and "shivalingam," reiterate the tree's symbolism.

[8] The cannonball tree is confused with the Sal *(Shorea robusta),* the tree whose flowers supposedly bloomed in unison when Gautama Buddha passed away and under which the previous Buddha Vessabhu attained enlightenment. The Bodhi tree under which Siddhartha Gautama reached enlightenment and became the Buddha is *Ficus religiosa.*

[9] In traditional medicine, the plant is used as a disinfectant, a microbicide, and an antidepressant. Said to have antibacterial, antiseptic, and analgesic qualities, the bark supposedly cures colds, the juice from its leaves is good for treating malaria and for skin diseases, chewing young leaves alleviates toothache, and the interior of the fruit can disinfect wounds. The pulp is sometimes fed to pigs and poultry to kill intestinal worms. See M.S. Shekhawat and M. Manokari, "In Vitro Propagation, Micromorphological Studies and Ex Vitro Rooting of Cannon Ball Tree (*Couroupita guianensis* aubl.): A Multipurpose Threatened Species," *Physiology and Molecular Biology of Plants* 22, no.1 (2016): 131–142.

[10] For an introduction to his work, see Lujan Matus's *The Art of Stalking Parallel Perception: The Living Tapestry of Lujan Matus*

(CreateSpace Independent Publishing Platform, 2015) and *Whisperings of the Dragon: Shamanic Practices to Awaken Your Primal Power* (CreateSpace Independent Publishing Platform, 2014). See also his website, Parallel Perception, www.parallelperception.com.

[11] See M. Marder, "Plant-Perceiving Is Plant-Thinking," *Los Angeles Review of Books Channel Blog* 2013, http://philosoplant.larevie wofbooks.org/?p=192.

Chapter H

[1] See Lujan Matus, *Whispering of the Dragon: Shamanic Techniques to Awaken Your Primal Power* (Createspace Independent Publishing Platform, 2014).

[2] See M. Gagliano, M. Grimonprez, M. Depczynski, and M. Renton, "Tuned In: Plant Roots Use Sound to Locate Water," *Oecologia* 184 (2017): 151–60.

[3] See M. Woods and A. Swartz Warren, *Glass Houses: A History of Greenhouses, Orangeries and Conservatories* (London: Aurum Press, 1988). See also a review of this book: Charles Hind, review of *Glass Houses,* by M. Woods and A. Swartz Warren, *Garden History* 16, no.2 (1988): 202–204.

[4]   A public, educational element was incorporated in the European botanic gardens only in the nineteenth century. On the surface, the promise was to reconnect the public with nature; however, the greenhouses served primarily for trialing and distributing plants of economic importance. Botanic gardens were institutions whose primary scientific endeavor was the so-called economic botany, the study and cultivation of plants for financial gain. It is now known that the greenhouses of the Royal Botanical Gardens, Kew, in London, for example, operated for this exact purpose, and in doing so, they played a crucial role in the expansion of the British Empire. See historical accounts in Lucille H. Brockway, *Science and Colonial Expansion: The Role of the British Royal Botanic Garden* (New Haven, CT: Yale University Press, 2002) and recent discussion by Z. Baber, "The Plants of Empire: Botanic Gardens, Colonial Power and Botanical Knowledge," *Journal of Contemporary Asia* 46, no.4 (2016): 659–679.

[5]   In a very energy-efficient way, plant roots grow from their tips by adding new cells through mitosis. The tip is the only part that moves in the soil, while the rest of the root body, made of mature cells, maintains contact with the soil by remaining stationary. See A. Sadeghi, A. Tonazzini, L. Popova, and B. Mazzolai, "A Novel Growing Device Inspired by Plant Root Soil

Penetration Behaviors," *PLoS ONE* 9, no.2 (2014): e90139.

[6] Scylla had six heads on long necks and twelve feet; she dwelled in a cave overlooking the strait and preyed on mariners who sailed by. On the other side of the strait, Charybdis lived under a fig tree near the shore and swallowed the sea three times a day, creating a dangerous whirlpool with shifting currents. Though Homer doesn't name the strait, later writers identified it as the Strait of Messina, the narrow channel between Sicily and the Italian mainland.

[7] In quantum mechanics, this idea of an object in one place "influencing" another far away—so that measuring one will determine the state of the other, regardless of the distance between them (i.e., they are described by the same mathematical relation known as a wave function)—came to be known as *entanglement*. Albert Einstein was troubled by this peculiar "nonlocal behavior" of particles (which he dubbed "spooky action at a distance") because it appeared to violate causality and, thus, be in conflict with one of the central tenets of relativity—information cannot be transmitted faster than the speed of light. In 1935, Einstein, Boris Podolsky, and Nathan Rosen introduced a thought experiment originally intended to demonstrate that such spooky action at a distance was impossible and that quantum theory

itself was either wrong or at least incomplete. The Einstein-Podolsky-Rosen (EPR) paradox, as it came to be known, was not resolved until 1964. See H. Nikolic, "EPR Before EPR: A 1930 Einstein-Bohr Thought Experiment Revisited," *European Journal of Physics* 33 (2012): 1089–1097.

[8]   See Donna J. Haraway's concept of *sympoiesis* (from the ancient Greek words *syn,* "together" and *poiesis,* "creation, making") in *Staying with the Trouble: Making Kin in the Chthulucene* (Durham, NC: Duke University Press, 2016), where she offers provocative new ways to reconfigure our relations to the earth and all its inhabitants.

Chapter A

[1]   Both known as "sequoias," coast redwoods and giant sequoias are, in fact, different species with different natural growing ranges. *Sequoia sempervirens,* coast redwoods, are the tallest known trees in the world and, as their common name suggests, they like growing in a relatively narrow strip of coastline of northern California, where the Pacific Ocean provides the perfect cooling and moistening conditions (including the notorious fog typical of the summer months) for these trees to thrive. *Sequoiadendron giganteum,* giant sequoias, are the most massive trees in

the world and are only found growing far inland and at altitude in the Sierra Nevada, where the dry mountain air and snowpack of the mountains provides them with the right conditions and especially the huge quantities of water they need to thrive.

[2] The core ideas of this lecture (M. Gagliano, "The Plant Revolution: And the Stories We Tell," lecture, National Bioneers Conference, San Rafael, CA, 2014) formed the basis of a short essay coauthored with philosopher Micheal Marder and published online that year: M. Gagliano and M. Marder, "What Plant Revolution Would You Opt For?" *The Philosopher's Plant—LA Reviews of Book* (blog), November 14, 2014. The essay was subsequently republished in M. Marder, *Grafts: Writings on Plants* (Minneapolis, MN: Univocal, 2017).

[3] See P.H. Abelson and P.J. Hines, "The Plant Revolution," *Science* 285, no.5426 (1999): 367–368.

[4] See M. Gagliano, "Seeing Green: The Re-Discovery of Plants and Nature's Wisdom," *Societies* 3 (2013): 147–157.

[5] Annuals are plants that complete the life cycle—from germination to flowering and the production of seeds—within one year and then die. Perennials are plants with a longer life cycle and, given proper conditions, can live for several

(or many) years. Modern industrialized agro-ecosystems grow perennial plants as annuals for convenience and profit.

[6] For an expanded discussion on this topic, see P. Gibson and M. Gagliano, "The Feminist Plant: Changing Relations with the Water Lily," *Ethics and the Environment* 22, no.2 (2017): 125–147.

[7] Research findings from this emerging approach to plants have been beautifully summarized by outstanding scientists such as Daniel Chamovitz and Richard Karban. See D. Chamovitz, *What a Plant Knows: a Field Guide to the Senses* (Scribe 2012); R. Karban, *Plant Sensing and Communication* (Chicago: Chicago University Press 2015). Interestingly, this field of research is moving so fast that even these relatively recent books are, in part, already out-of-date, in that some things they identified as unknown are no longer unknown.

[8] According to the definition in Art. 2 of the Convention on Biological Diversity, the term *biotechnology* refers to "any technological application that uses biological systems, living organisms, or derivatives thereof, to make or modify products or processes for specific use."

[9] Clearly, the same question applies to animals and all other living organisms.

[10]   For an interesting exploration of this topic, see Michael Hauskeller, *Biotechnology and the Integrity of Life: Taking Public Fears Seriously* (Aldershot, U.K.: Ashgate, 2007).

[11]   The fact that our brain operates on multiple dimensions, not just the three dimensions that we are accustomed to, was recently demonstrated by a group of European neuroscientists. They discovered a universe of multidimensional geometrical structures and spaces within the networks of the brain with up to eleven dimensions. See M.W. Reimann, M. Nolte, M. Scolamiero, K. Turner, R. Perin, G. Chindemi, P. Dlotko et al., "Cliques of Neurons Bound into Cavities Provide a Missing Link Between Structure and Function," *Frontiers in Computational Neuroscience* 11 (2017): 48.

[12]   Aside from its well-known presence in sci-fi literature, cinema, and games, the word *portal* is used here as an equivalent to the cosmological concept of wormhole—the space-time curvature connecting two distant locations allowed by Einstein's theory of general relativity—in modern theoretical physics. I am in no way able to provide a physicist's (or a philosopher's) explanation for what occurred in the redwood forest simply because I am no physicist (or philosopher). While theoretical physicist colleagues are still speculating on whether it is truly possible for wormholes to

actually exist (and what their properties may actually be), my experience of the space-time curvature allows for the existence of such phenomenon to be possible. As a scientist, I am reporting here direct observations and "field data" as a contribution to this research area of enquiry.

[13] The neutron fluxes originating at the Earth's surface are background emissions constantly transforming the microstructure of the planet's crust. These are fluxes of "slow neutrons" with energies in the range of a few electronvolts or a few fractions of an electronvolt (eV). The ultra-weak energy of these slow-moving neutrons is distributed in the form of non-ionizing radiation (mostly heat), which induces strong biological responses in living organisms but causes no radiation damage to their biological macromolecules (e.g., proteins). Abnormal spikes in these slow neutron fluxes have been observed at certain times (in conjunction with lunar periodicity and seismic activity) and in relation to various ecological assemblages (e.g., mixed forests). In the context of ecosystems, the presence of long-lasting spikes depends on the number and composition of species in the community and is characterized by specific time (seasonal) variations. Research findings by scientists at the Russian Academy of Sciences indicate that

spatial-temporal variations in these neutron fluxes may be involved in shaping various landscapes and harmonizing natural communities; the phenomenon may play a major role in the maintenance of the microclimate as well as the perception of and response to astrogeophysical events by living organisms. Note that the high-energy neutrons that damage materials and whose ionizing radiations are highly hazardous to biological systems are known as "fast neutrons" and usually have energies between 0.1 and 3 million electronvolts (MeV) and speeds of 14,000km/s, or higher. They are different from the "slow neutrons" that characterize these fluxes. I became aware of this area of research through inspiring discussions with Australian geophysicist, Dr. Tom Chalko, in 2016.

[14]   See Vanessa Ogle, *The Global Transformation of Time: 1870–1950* (Cambridge, MA: Harvard University Press, 2015).

[15]   Recently, two American professors proposed to remove all time zones and switch the whole world to one "Coordinated Universal Time" (UTC). UTC would set every watch across the world to the exact same time—Greenwich Mean Time in London, to be precise—regardless of the sun's position in the sky. The proponents claim that UTC would save money and time, thereby facilitating business transactions and

commercial activities. The two professors also proposed a new calendar, the Henry-Hanke calendar, which would make financial calculations simpler. It seems that applied economics is the *only* consideration on the agenda, further aligning time as "out there," a commodity for the exclusive interest of commerce and a powerful centralizing force of global control.

[16] The Buddhist concept of *samsara* encapsulates and explains very well the human condition of ignorance.

[17] Over the years, there has been one particular plant who has provided me with the deep and authentic experience of time "in here," hence reaffirming my multidimensionality as a human being over and over again. I was fortunate to encounter this plant several years ago in the most pristine and reverent ceremonial settings. The plant supports focus, insight, and an authentic connection to your own heart and heart's intelligence. The plant is *Theobroma cacao,* and Catherine and Willow Francis are the hearts offering it in the form of a concentrated, pure, and traditionally prepared drink, as part of the ceremony I have been privileged to be part of. Willow and Catherine were initiated in this work long before it became a fashionable thing to play with, and they have continually been guided and

re-initiated by the plant spirit himself ever since; this has enabled them to rest in a space of great reverence to facilitate a unique and powerful inner journey experience. See www.cacaoceremonies.com and www.reverencechocolate.com.au.

[18] See Andrea Morris, "A Mind Without a Brain: The Science of Plant Intelligence Takes Root" *Forbes,* May 9, 2018.

Coda M

[1] The ability of a baby to close her fist around anything that is placed in the tiny palm is known as the *palmar grasp reflex* and is one of the most important infantile reflexes. This reflex first appears at sixteen weeks' gestation. See Y. Futagi, Y. Toribe, and Y. Suzuki, "The Grasp Reflex and Moro Reflex in Infants: Hierarchy of Primitive Reflex Responses," *International Journal of Pediatrics* 12 (2012): 191562.

[2] As I researched the information I had received during the *dieta* with Tobacco, I came across a paper on the first physical evidence of tobacco in Mayan culture, which confirmed what the plant had already shared with me. See D.V. Zagorevski and J.A. Loughmiller-Newman, "The Detection of Nicotine in a Late Mayan Period Flask by Gas Chromatography and Liquid Chromatography Mass Spectrometry Methods,"

Rapid Communication in Mass Spectrometry 26 (2012): 403–411; see also Francis Robicsek, *The Smoking Gods: Tobacco in Maya Art, History, and Religion* (Norman: University of Oklahoma Press, 1978).

[3] He also indicated that his medicine alleviated conditions that affected muscles due to the malfunctioning of mitochondria. At the time, I had no idea that something called "mitochondrial disease" actually existed. As I started researching the information received from the plant, I learned that fatigue and weakness of the musculature of the chest wall and diaphragm are common manifestations of mitochondrial disease.

[4] For example, when we sing in unison, like in choirs, our heart rates tend to synchronize and beat as one, with positive effects on well-being and health. See B. Vickhoff, H. Malmgren, R. Åström, G. Nyberg, S.-R. Ekström, M. Engwall, J. Snygg et al., "Music Structure Determines Heart Rate Variability of Singers," *Frontiers in Psychology* 4 (2013): 334.

ACKNOWLEDGMENTS

The writing of this book commenced in June 2016. Six months earlier, my academic career had come to a sudden and terrifying halt as my research funding ran dry and my university position as a research associate professor was turned into the empty accolade of "adjunct senior fellow" with no lab and no office. In other words, I was left unemployed and, as I would come to appreciate over time, unemployable. (My research fit in no preconceived disciplinary box, and neither did I.)

During the following two years, I discovered that life requires a little budget but a great deal of generosity from the people around you. I was blessed by a small savings account and the titanic flood of bigheartedness, kindness, and support I received from many, without whom this book would have never sprouted into the light of day. I owe a special debt of gratitude to Martial Depczynski and Damian Hadchiti, who openhandedly gave me a place to call home at no cost, at a time when any amount would have been too much. I am particularly grateful to my three research assistants: Nili Duvdevani and Mavra Grimonprez, the two special women who, at different times over the years, gifted me with their hands-on support so that the massive tasks set by my research could be actually accomplished, and Picasso, the extraordinary dog who kept me smiling always, especially when I felt overwhelmed, tired, or disheartened, and who thus made the impossible possible.

And as I embarked on the writing journey, many held me with gentle care, keeping me emotionally buoyant and inspired, helped me brainstorm ideas for a book-to-be, and encouraged me all the way until that book-to-be came into being: Francesca Berti and Fulvio Trombotto, Frauke Sandig and Eric Black, Sa and Claudio Silvano, Catherine and Willow Francis, Lujan and Mizpah Matus, Alex Pelizzon, Sarah Laborde, Deanna Foster, Chiara Pazzano, January Truscheit, and my family. Special thanks to Patrizia Gajaschi, who made each chapter beautiful with her artwork, and once again, to Martial Depczynski, who read and edited all the chapters as they materialized onto the computer screen in their own random order and helped me define, clarify, and make sense of the ideas I was trying to express.

Much gratitude to the numerous and incredible friends in Adelaide, Sydney, and on the Hawaiian Islands for their heartfelt support, despite the many miles that separate us. Those who were witnesses to this journey will also know that some people who played major roles in this story are patently missing from these pages or their name concealed. They were omitted or veiled on purpose to protect them and their lives; you know who you are and know that I love you, always.

A special mention must be made of the entire team at North Atlantic Books and particularly my publisher, Tim McKee, who saw the potential within me when I had no interest whatsoever in writing a book (that was years before I would consider authoring one) and welcomed me when that time arrived, understanding what this book was all about, and believing in and supporting me. Thanks also to my editors, Alison Knowles and Louis Swaim, for all their work (especially all their behind-the-scenes labor!) in making sure things unfolded smoothly, and Jennifer Eastman, for her magic touches with the copyediting process of this book.

And, last but not least, this book owes its largest debt to the vegetal kingdom expressed in all places and all forms, through whom I directly experienced the meaning of interconnectedness and by whom I am continually taught how to be a truly integrated and openhearted human in the world. Life on this beloved Earth is a truly marvelous event—I am so grateful for this incredible experience of being life. I wish that you too encounter your own wonder and its timeless enchantment, that you too realize the pure joy that lives inside the luminous, powerful, and mysterious being that you are, as you breathe in and out in the clear sky of your infinite heart.

Resources and Useful Links

Frauke Sandig and Eric Black, Umbrella Films—www.
umbrellafilms.org

Sa and Claudio Silvano, Sacred Radiance—www.sacre
dradiance.net

Catherine and Willow Francis, Reverence Chocolate—w
ww.reverencechocolate.com.au

Lujan Matus, Parallel Perception—www.parallelpercept
ion.com

Mizpah Matus, Raw Food Solutions—www.rawfoodsolu
tion.com

Valerie DeJose, The Vestibule Center For Sound
Living—www.sound-living.com

ABOUT THE AUTHOR AND THE CONTRIBUTING ARTIST

The Author

© MANU THEOBALD

Monica Gagliano is research associate professor of evolutionary ecology and former fellow of the Australian Research Council (2012–2015). She is currently a research affiliate at the Environment Institute at the University of Sydney and holds an adjunct position as senior research fellow at the Centre for Evolutionary Biology at the University of Western Australia. She is the author of numerous scientific articles in the fields of animal and plant behavioral and evolutionary ecology and is the coeditor (with Patrícia Vieira and John Ryan) of *The Green Thread: Dialogues with the Vegetal World* and *The Language of Plants: Science, Philosophy and Literature,* and (with Frantisek Baluska and Guenther Witzany) *Memory and*

Learning in Plants. An innovative scientist, Gagliano has pioneered the brand-new research field of plant bioacoustics, for the first time experimentally demonstrating that plants emit their own "voices" and, moreover, detect and respond to the sounds of their environments. Her work has extended the concept of cognition (including perception, learning processes, memory, and consciousness) in plants. By demonstrating experimentally that learning, memory, and decision-making are not the exclusive province of animals, she has reignited the discourse on plant subjectivity and ethical and legal standing. Inspired by encounters with nature and with indigenous elders from around the world, Gagliano is not only transforming our perception of plants but also of our very nature. Her science is based on a progressive and holistic approach to science—one that is comfortable engaging at the interface between areas as diverse as ecology, physics, law, anthropology, philosophy, literature, music and the arts, and spirituality. By rekindling a sense of wonder for this beautiful place we call home, she is helping to create a fresh imaginative ecology of mind that can inspire the emergence of truly innovative solutions to human relations with the world we coinhabit. For more information, visit www.monicagagliano.com.

The Illustrator

Patrizia Gajaschi is a Mexican artist based in Australia. After completing her studies in international relations in Italy and spending some years working in nongovernmental organizations, she had a life-changing experience in Peru while working with indigenous communities, after which she spent the next seven years traveling the world. Currently she lives in Sydney, where she shares her love by teaching yoga and creating art, along with running a business selling yoga accessories. For more information, visit www.pattygajaschi.com.

BLACK-AND-WHITE ARTWORK FEATURED IN THIS BOOK

CHAPTER O, "Heart," 2017

The heart symbolizes life and connection, both expressed by a unique line representing the continuum between the two worlds.

CHAPTER R, "Mandala," 2017

The open eye represents a conscious and awakened being sharing the sound of the cosmos for those ones who are ready to listen.

CHAPTER Y, "Leaf," 2017

Like the palm of a hand, the palm of the leaf tells a story: we don't really know what those lines are revealing. We just need to trust that they will eventually lead us to our heart.

CHAPTER N, "Spiral," 2018

Remembering is not a linear process but a spiral, where we need to come back again and again before we are able to let go of our conditioned perspective.

CHAPTER G, "Eye," 2017

The eye that knows how to see in the dark knows how to find the light.

CHAPTER H, "Wind Rose," 2017

The wind rose represents the range of choices and possibilities available to humanity; it is up to our heart to choose the wellbeing of the whole.

CHAPTER A, "Unalome," 2017

Time and space are not linear concepts; they expand and contract in a harmonic movement, where the lines leading to our heart eventually meet and show us the right path.

CODA M, "Hand," 2018

Do you remember now? It was in your hand.

About North Atlantic Books

North Atlantic Books (NAB) is an independent, nonprofit publisher committed to a bold exploration of the relationships between mind, body, spirit, and nature. Founded in 1974, NAB aims to nurture a holistic view of the arts, sciences, humanities, and healing. To make a donation or to learn more about our books, authors, events, and newsletter, please visit www.northatlanticbooks.com.

***

North Atlantic Books is the publishing arm of the Society for the Study of Native Arts and Sciences, a 501(c)(3) nonprofit educational organization that promotes cross-cultural perspectives linking scientific, social, and artistic fields. To learn how you can support us, please visit our website.